Bright Light

Spiritual Lessons from a Life in Acting

D0037170

Bright Light

Spiritual Lessons from a Life in Acting

Dee Wallace with John Nelson

BOOKS

Winchester, UK
Washington, USA

First published by O-Books, 2011
O-Books is an imprint of John Hunt Publishing Ltd., Laurel House, Station Approach,
Alresford, Hants, SO24 9JH, UK
office1@o-books.net
www.o-books.com

For distributor details and how to order please visit the 'Ordering' section on our website.

Text copyright: Dee Wallace 2010

ISBN: 978 1 84694 598 4

A CIP catalogue record for this book is available from the British Library.

Design: Tom Davies

Printed in the UK by CPI Antony Rowe
Printed in the USA by Offset Paperback Mfrs, Inc

We operate a distinctive and ethical publishing philosophy in all
areas of our business, from our global network of authors to
production and worldwide distribution.

CONTENTS

Preface   xi
Acknowledgments   xiii

Chapter One: The Journey Starts with Intention   1
Chapter Two: The Art of Beingness   17
Chapter Three: The High-Energy Zone   31
Chapter Four: Judgment Day   47
Chapter Five: The Instinctive Response   63
Chapter Six: The Heart Light   77
Chapter Seven: Sending Heart Energy   91
Chapter Eight: The Immaculate Reception   105
Chapter Nine: The Zero Point   117
Chapter Ten: Surrender   131
Chapter Eleven: Just Know   149
Chapter Twelve: I AM   165
Appendix
1. Intention   177
2. Beingness   179
3. High Energy   181
4. Judgment   183
5. Instinct   185
6. Heart   187
7. Sending Out   189
8. Reception   191
9. Zero Point   193
10. Surrender   195
11. Knowing   196
12. I AM   197

Bibliography   198
About the Authors   199

This is my story.
And yours.
We are born with our light.
The world challenges that light.
Either we keep it shining or we don't.

This book is dedicated to Charles Conrad and his passion for truth in every moment; to Christopher Stone, my soul mate, with whom my healing journey began; and to my beloved Gram Bow, my best friend, confidante, and support.

Preface

When I channel healing sessions and teach seminars, I always use myself and by extension my life as examples of how we get stuck subconsciously in creating the lives we want. I also receive feedback from participants regarding how I, as an 'actor and movie star,' think I need to heal. Aren't I successful and happy now?

It was natural for me to bring the journey of my life as an actor together with the healing principles I know so well. I wanted to express 'every man's' journey of life: innocence, awakening, loss of self, the journey of truth, and re-awakening. And I wanted to explore it through the experiences of the acting world: a perfect metaphor for the illusion of 'life.' The purpose, if one must have a purpose other than joy, was to share the experience and journey of finding my light, my happiness, and myself in life. Like a good movie, I am hoping this story of me helps you relate to the story of you. Our light never goes out: we simply dim it because we react to life and stop choosing. We forget we're special. We don't remember we are the greater whole.

I have also included metaphysical topics in an appendix for the purpose of clarifying the 'lessons' I was experiencing in each of the chapters. Originally, each was placed at the end of the chapter to which it related. I leave to your discretion whether you choose to read the text and save the topics for last, or refer to them as you move through the book. Either way, they succinctly state the concepts we all experience through this wonderful movie called 'life.'

Writing this book was often painful when long-buried memories were brought up and re-experienced. Some of it was frustrating, going back through and reliving the blocks and confusion I seemingly had no power over at the time. Much of it was cathartic, unexplainable love and joy. My hope is, when you arrive at its completion, you know that you, too, are the author of your own story. Only you can choose the chapters, the transitions, and the finale. Only you.

Acknowledgments

There are so many incredible energies that encouraged me to write this book. Here, I am celebrating the few that actually took it into physical form.

I am extremely grateful to Barbara Neighbors Deal, my agent and cheerleader. It was Barbara who, many years ago, saw the potential in a very raw book called *Conscious Creation*, agreed to guide and nurture me, and lead me to amazing souls who would be instrumental in its final completion. She never gave up, and has supported me in this second journey with *Bright Light*.

I am also deeply, deeply indebted to John Nelson for his professional contribution to the writing of *Bright Light*. Without John's superb editing, the book simply would not have been written with such a succinct, organized, and directed vision. John's uncanny ability to take an elusive creative idea and create a solid direction of coherent storytelling is often incomprehensible to me in its clarity. And after each session with him, the direction was so clear and focused that my channel effortlessly opened and created. It was nothing short of magical. It is my belief that this book could not have been written without him, and my honor to include his name on the cover. We were, in every sense, partners in this creative endeavor.

And lastly, I pay homage to my wonderful soul mate, Christopher Stone, who, through the readings with medium John Edward, encouraged me to never give up.

And to my mentor, Charles Conrad, who changed and enlightened my life in miraculous ways.

Chapter One

The Journey Starts with Intention

Dear Daddy,
I wish you wouldn't be drunk. I wish you wouldn't yell at Mommy
so much like you're gonna hit her. It scares Damon and me. I really
love you when you're nice, Daddy. You're such a good daddy then.
I like when you dance with me. Please don't drink so I can love you.
Deanna (Age 8)

I love where I come from: the state of Kansas and a certain state of mind. I love my family and cherish my upbringing despite all its turmoil and poverty. I love the values that I was raised with, but there were also many conflicting messages: you can/you can't, you're safe/it's dangerous. These messages came from strong, intelligent people, who were also damaged and flawed: my mother, and my maternal and paternal grandmothers, and my conflicted alcoholic father. My paternal grandmother, Gram Bow as we called her, was my primary caretaker because I had a 'working mother.' She was also the primary caretaker of our church. For Kansans of that era, the church was the most fundamental institution of both secular and spiritual belief. Gram Bow was a grand dame of the matriarchal society that was the Washington Avenue Methodist Church, where I received my spiritual upbringing.

On the maternal side, Grandma Nichols was Southern Baptist and much stricter, and fearful of a God full of fire and brimstone. Joyfulness was not a part of her religious beliefs from my young perspective. And this created a conflict. For instance, my mother would take me to dance lessons while instructing me, 'Don't tell Grandma.' This was one of the first negative messages that impinged on my growing creative self and my firm intention to 'be me,' while fending off the fearful judgments of others. And then there was my father who didn't practice religion at all. His favorite quote was, 'I don't have to go to church to believe in God.' So many mixed messages growing up: spirituality and religion, and how that was interwoven into your being, whom you became, and what you dared to do in the world: be you, but please them.

Mother was always my best mentor. She was my guidance, my strength, and my moral backbone. She was a brilliant community actress and my first acting teacher. In Kansas she performed as a 'hobby' while she worked as a secretary to support the family. I grew up watching her entertain the local music groups, the mayor and other prominent citizens, perform in community and religious plays, and give half-hour readings at our church. I watched her live her passion on weekends only. The first time I can truly remember wanting to creatively affect people with my light was while watching my mother presenting her famous annual dramatic reading, 'The Crucifixion,' at our church. It was a thrilling thirty-minute piece that replaced the sermon on Palm Sunday. Churchgoers from four states came to see my mother perform, and as I looked around the packed church I saw people weeping, and I said to myself, Wow ... my mom did this; my mom moved these people. The moment stunned me. It ignited within me the remembrance of my bright light and its destiny. If it had been a scene in a movie, they would have done a close-up on my little-girl face, eyes wide with acknowledgment and awe, looking up at adults riveted and moved by my mother's perfor-mance. I was eight years old, and I realized the power of creativity: the healing power of talent when it springs from one's truth. That intention to be truthful creatively was instilled in me in that moment. But my mother also owned an intention to 'keep it small,' one I never wanted to share.

Looking back on that little girl, I realize that I just came in, as we all do, as this beautiful light; and I knew I wanted that light to

shine: that was my job this lifetime. That is what we're all here to
do: shine our light. I wanted to be a great dancer and a movie
star and Miss America. But I was afraid to totally commit myself
to that intention – God might not approve of my grandiose
vision. Even the liberal Methodists weren't sure about my
wanting to be big and important and wealthy – everyone was
very big on humility. I began to wonder how my bright light and
inbred sense of humility could coexist harmoniously. I loved my
light. I didn't want to turn it down. And somehow, it never lost
its glow throughout my childhood, even with all the confusing
religious messages and my father's drinking and his ultimate
suicide and our wretched poverty.

We never had enough money. Daddy couldn't hold down a
job and Mom could barely support us as a secretary. So I was
elected to deal with the steady stream of bill collectors. Cute and
vulnerable, I would answer the door and lie, 'Mommy and
Daddy aren't home, but I'll give them the message.' I hated to lie.
I still do. It makes me feel dirty.

But, while we may have been destitute, we were not impoverished spiritually – there is a difference. Because despite such
lack, I felt a huge amount of love, encouragement, and opportunity. And somehow, all of that support helped me keep my
light shining. The obvious path was to use my talent to help take
care of my family. I modeled to make money. I was thrilled when
my dad arranged for me to be the 'Dell Comic Queen.' Daddy
worked for a brief time for Dell Comics, then a subsidiary of Walt
Disney Studios. He was actually a salesman but incredibly
creative. He managed to become involved in the publicity side
somehow, and I became the 'Dell Comic Queen' and made
appearances with Gene Autry, Walt Disney, and other celebrities.
I wore a cheesy little cardboard crown with glitter, but I got to
ride in parades and pretend I was a beauty queen. I booked
commercials. It all made me so happy and it helped pay the bills.
My creative happy self allowed me to take care of the people I

loved, and in doing so I knew they would take care of me and I would be safe. And so began the quest of my lifetime: knowing I was safe in this world while being my authentic self. My light shone bright while I clung to my passion. And all of a sudden what I was doing was okay with everyone, even with Grandma Nichols. I was serving others, after all, so God must be happy too. I sure was. I was in my joy and shining brightly, and I was so loved; it seemed like it was all just meant to be.

Despite all of the challenges, the overall message coming from my family was how special I was: I could do amazing things in this life. We would sit around and watch the Hit Parade, and my dad would get up and dance with me, and he'd say, 'Button-nose, you're so talented. You could be on that show one day.' And we'd watch the Miss America Pageant, and my dad with tears in his eyes would say, 'You can do that; you're beautiful and talented.' Nobody ever told me that I could be president, but everyone said I could be a creative force in this world. Yes, that was what I was made to do. I was just born to be creative: be it singing, dancing, arts and crafts, or writing. I loved writing poetry. And I used to just live for Monday nights, because that was my dance class. I would wait expectantly for that one thrilling acting lesson each month. Any time I was able to move into my creativity, I felt at home, I felt safe, I knew I belonged. When I walked into math or science class, I knew I didn't belong there. But give me something creative, and my light shone bright. My intention to be 'me' was very clear from my first spark of consciousness.

Like all children, I had an ability to merge with my creation, to become one with it. It became me, and I was it. Often the power of this embodiment was too much for some people to handle. I remember a high school speech contest: I recited a dramatic reading that today would win me an Academy Award! The notes from the judge said that 'I went into the material so much and became so emotionally committed that it made him feel uneasy.' I watched as my beloved drama teacher's face dissolved into disappointment. I had been his chance to take the state championship. Again, here was the message about being too powerful. I think about that now and wonder how that episode didn't totally discourage me. But I held on to what I knew. My job was to open my heart so I could open up everybody else's heart, just as my mom did that day in the sanctuary. I just always knew that was the true power of creativity.

That feedback did, however, reinforce my fear of being judged. How can you make your truthfulness smaller? Again, that bright-light/humility conflict reared up. I was always raised to be brutally truthful, to say what I thought and be who I was, and take that into all of my creative endeavors. But, at the same time, I was to be very cautious of what other people thought of me. I was hearing two entirely different messages: Be yourself, but also be what they want (or you'll get judged). Don't park outside with your boyfriend – what will the neighbors think? Say what you think, but in a respectful way that won't offend people. Make sure you dress appropriately and use the correct language, because people might get the wrong impression. My intention of shining brightly and their intention of keeping me safe – or was it under control? – collapsed together.

In high school I went through a period where I was growing too fast and would get mini seizures which would make me faint. The doctor assured us that this was really quite natural and that a lot of kids go through these growth spurts. He gave me some medicine and sent me off to school.

In hushed tones, my mother told me, 'Deanna, don't tell anybody about this; nobody is supposed to know,' which made me feel dirty and unsafe. The message again: You won't be accepted; you're not okay, and they'll judge you. This message of having to be safe at any cost was clouding my intention to 'be me.' My family literally embodied this dichotomy. My paternal grandmother, Gram Bow, was an artist. She had been a painter and was very ballsy and 'out there' for a woman from her gener-

5

ation. She embraced creativity for women, while men were supposed to work. My maternal grandmother was very soft-spoken, very fearful of God and the consequences of sin. She raised five children, giving them a strict religious upbringing. To me, it was sinful that I was forced to keep my dancing a secret from her. So, here I have the greatest joy in my life, dancing – which my mother not only allowed but encouraged – and we couldn't tell her mother for fear of judgment. Again, there was this fear of being judged for the truthfulness of my creativity, and yet I knew that was where I had to live. My mother could use her creativity 'as a hobby'; but Daddy, who was also sensitive and creative, had to disown his softness and talent to survive in this cookie-cutter world.

People ask me why I became an actor. I had no choice. I was compelled by my inner being, which knew without question that my joy, truthfulness and creativity was the authentic me. I had to express my creativity. I originally wanted to be a dancer and was a soloist with two ballet companies, but I never really had the physique to be a ballerina. So I turned my creative expression to what I knew next: acting. I would move people as my mother had done. Again, my good family message was that I could do this. I was just urged to do it in Kansas, where I was 'safe.' It was a constant challenge for discernment: my truth versus the 'truths' of the other gods in my life. For instance, there was the belief that you had to work really, really hard – that Midwest work ethic – or you were not going to get there. And yet when I went into my creative life, everything seemed so easy; everything just flowed for me. I was free, and nothing was hard. Whenever I was taken out of this flow, I really clamored to get it back. It was pure joy. I could celebrate me.

I remember taking a horrible hit energetically one day. We were coming home from a dance recital. I was in the back seat and my aunt was with us, and we were talking about the recital and I joyfully exclaimed, 'Mom, I was good. I was really, really good!' I had so much joy and happiness that I had moved people.

My aunt turned around and berated me: 'Deanna, don't be so full of yourself. Nice little girls don't brag about themselves. Shame on you.' Shame, indeed. 'You need to be more humble than that.'

I can feel the sting of it now even as I write about it. It was as if a stake had been shoved through my heart. The life was pulled out of me. In one instant I fell from my glorious and joyful state of knowing, and succumbed to that fear of being wrongly judged for being me. It was such a tiny moment, an almost insignificant moment. But I got the message. It's not okay to know you're good. It's not okay to love and celebrate yourself. You're not safe to love yourself. It just zapped the joy right out of me. It planted a seed right then, and I made a decision: I would turn down my creative flame, so it couldn't be snuffed out like that again. I was choosing a life of vigilant caution. Of course, that limits your experience and creation in life. You no longer shout, 'I am great, I am wonderful, I am passionate, and I am creative bliss!' I've been working to reclaim all of that joy ever since. And it was that pure sense of knowing and loving me that created everything so effortlessly. I just had to hold on to my intention of Being Me.

Sometimes, it was all an overwhelming challenge. I had been nominated for Homecoming Queen, but couldn't bear the thought of my father staggering up to the podium where we would all stand to receive the results.

I went to him and said, 'Daddy, can you promise me you won't drink that day? If you don't drink, I want you to escort me.' He looked at me through already half-blitzed eyes. It was 4:00 P.M.

He took a deep breath. 'Sorry, Button-nose, I can't promise that.'

I turned and ran to my room. It hurt that the bottle was more important to him than I was. I wanted to stand proud and feel special as the little girl who danced with her daddy on Saturday nights to the Hit Parade. I won Homecoming Queen, but it was bittersweet. A few months later, Daddy took his own life. Emotionally and psychologically I was a wreck. It forced me to just give up fighting and allow the energy to move through me, to be in the flow. I had no direction, and a dimmed light. My mother insisted that I go to college so I would be 'safe in our changing world.' I knew by this time that I wasn't going to be a major dancer, and started looking into other avenues of creative expression. I enrolled at the University of Kansas and majored in theater and English education. Acting classes were a part of this curriculum. I felt that familiar flicker of my light yearning to ignite its passion again. But I was to be disappointed. In acting class they would run through exercises – boring acting exercises done over and over again. I felt nothing resonate. It's like that song from *A Chorus Line*: 'Okay, how often do I have to pretend to be a snowflake? Is this really what acting is all about?' It annoyed the hell out of me.

Breaking scenes down into 'beats' to know exactly what you were going to do next would just take the joy out of the moment for me. When I left the energy of blind trust and began mentally controlling the outcome, my performance suffered. This didn't make sense to most actors, or teachers for that matter. For them, the more you studied your part and the more you figured it out and the more answers you had, the more you were on 'safe' ground. And it worked for them. Brilliantly. But I knew my knowingness was in not knowing. It was in being and flowing in that absolute moment of joy. It was there I was safe.

College was a very difficult time for me. How could I be free and responsible at the same time? I had to commute from Kansas City to Lawrence, Kansas. I was taking on a huge study load three days a week, and working full time two days a week to pay my way through school. It was difficult to perform in student productions at the university because I couldn't make all the rehearsals. I started working in the Kansas City community theater. I joyfully joined the cast of *Who's Afraid of Virginia Woolf?* and it was my first experience of successfully combining rehearsals with its scene breakdown approach, and being in the moment. I learned how to work on a play, to think and talk things through with the director and with the actors, form an acting intention; and yet trust, let go, and be in the moment when I walked out on that stage. I could 'be' Honey.

Opening night, the director came back afterward and asked, 'My God, what happened to you up there?'

I felt myself panic a little. Is this a judgment? 'What do you mean?' I stammered.

'Well, it's like she just took you over – you were her. What happened? I didn't see that in rehearsals.' My heart soared.

I was starting to learn about using energy: how to direct it with intention and let it go simultaneously. I just didn't know it consciously. If you know where you want to go in a scene – your 'acting intention' – and then bring in that energy of excitement and joy, it all comes together in a spontaneous and sometimes unpredictable way. I was reborn as an actor. There was hope for my natural approach to acting. Years later, I would come to discover an acting technique that was literally based on that concept. But this was my first acknowledgment that my head and my heart could work together on this crazy ride of acting from my authentic self. What I didn't know then was that the same principles apply to life: I can create an intention or a plan to reach a goal, but then release it and allow my greater energy to flow through me and create what it will.

This whole form/flow concept was so empowering. Acting became very exciting for me, and I started performing in a lot of local theater, which at that time was a really great venue. I was practicing how to combine form and freedom into one creation. Earlier I had a false belief: form limited creation! Now I could redefine that belief. I never liked to create formulas or figure everything out. Ergo, my failings in math and science. That was not how my creative mind worked. But now I was open to the possibility that form could lead ultimately to freedom, or the avenue to express myself creatively.

College allowed me to grow up and own my power. I did more local plays, taught a year of high school, and then charged off and never looked back. That light kept getting bigger and brighter. I knew I had to move on, to claim my future. It was an 'I have to' dictate. It wasn't like: Well, maybe I will. It was: My authentic self has to do this, and if not now, when? Well, 'Ask and you will receive.' Since I had never been out of Kansas, I wasn't sure where to start. So I picked up the *New York Times* in the school library, and there was an article about Hal Prince, who was the biggest producer on Broadway. He was looking for an unknown to star in his new musical, which was ultimately called *A Little Night Music*. So I wrote him a letter and had my brother's friend take some headshots. Talk about naive! I said, 'Mr Prince, I'm from Kansas and I'm coming to New York. Just think of the publicity – a newcomer from Kansas.' I wish I had a copy of that letter. Three weeks later, I got a call from his secretary. Mr Prince would like to fly me to NY to audition for *A Little Night Music*.

Well, being raised the honest, straightforward girl that I was, I said, 'Oh wow, that's great, but I already have a ticket.' I could have gotten a first-class seat and the whole nine yards. You just can't take the Kansas out of the girl, as they say. Sometimes that helped me keep my intention clear.

Two months later I was off to New York City in search of fame and fortune. I arrived at the airport, had a taxi drop my belongings off at the studio apartment that I had rented, and I was off to Rockefeller Center to audition for Hal Prince. If you put this story in a movie, nobody would believe it! I got down to the last five girls after the dancing and acting auditions. Then Mr Prince came into the theater to hear us sing.

'I don't have a song; I didn't know I was going to have to sing,' I said rather weakly. Silence.

His assistant replied, 'Well, dear, this *is* a musical.' So on my first day in NYC, I sang 'Happy Birthday' off key and quite badly for the biggest producer on Broadway. I didn't get the part, obviously, but it got me to New York and I was on my way. And I made a lot of connections that day. I learned two very important lessons from this episode: be informed and be prepared. It helps carry the intention.

After that, one opportunity led to the next for me. Seriously, I think I succeeded so quickly in my career because I was so naive and trusting, and all kinds of people rushed forward to help me. Naiveté brings innocence and a lack of fear. You just have a trust in the Universe and that you're going to be taken care of, no matter what and who you are, or whatever the circumstances. And that is the purest intention one can have, and the dictum that many successful people have followed. I met girls at that audition who told me with whom to study. I met a guy at a coffee shop who looked at me and said, 'Are you an actress?'

'Yeah,' I said. 'I just got here from Kansas.'

'Come on,' he said. 'Somebody did this for me and I'm going to do this for you.' In three hours he gave me all the rules of the game for surviving in the New York acting world. He took me to buy some maps. He took me to get the directory to all the casting offices. He helped me to get signed up with an answering service. He told me the rules. 'You check that answering service every two hours.' He was right. You would get a call and they would say, 'Be there in forty-five minutes.' And if you hadn't checked in, you missed out on the audition. The Universe just brought the people to me or me to the people that I needed to meet. I have been vigilant to always 'pay it forward' to the next newbie.

I met a guy at an open call, and he took me to a Halloween party, and his agents were there. At the end of the night, they said, 'Dee, we think you ought to meet with us.'

I said, 'Great. What do you do?' Well, they were just some of the top agents in NY, and they signed me. I arrived there in

August, and this was Halloween. I had $4.06 left in my checking account. Three weeks later, I booked my first national commercial. I turned around and smiled and made $30,000. The new kid from Kansas was, as they say, happy-go-lucky.

And yet a strange thing began to happen. The more money I made, the more fearful I became of not making any more, and losing it if I did. It was the first time I had a savings account, and it excited me no end to deposit money into it. But my attitude was very unbalanced: I also didn't want to spend any of it. I just wanted to save the money. There was that safety net again. It was weird that I couldn't figure out how to do both. I must admit that the whole money thing has always been my greatest challenge. Later I sought help from a financial advisor who suggested a wonderful psychologist who specialized in money issues. It ended up that he helped me in a lot of other ways, too. I am still indebted to him for his invaluable guidance.

And the help kept coming. Another friend said, 'If you're going to be in NY, you have to study with Uta Hagen.' She was a great actress and teacher who owned the Berghof Studio with her husband Herbert Berghof. He said to me, 'You're not going to get accepted the first time – I'm going in for my fourth audition – but I'll do the scene with you if you want to audition.' We got there at 4:00 A.M. to stand in line just to sign up for the privilege of auditioning for Uta Hagen. He asked me what scene I was doing for my audition. I chose one from a little play called *Mary, Mary* that I did in Kansas City.

'You can't do a scene like that for Uta Hagen. You have to do a classic, like Tennessee Williams or William Inge.' But I had been really good in that play, and I knew and liked it, and that's the scene I did. That ability to stick to what feels right, even though someone more knowledgeable disagrees, has always been a part of me from childhood. Some people called it stubborn. I called it authentic. I knew I was ready, and was comfortable in that part. He said, 'Okay, I'll go in with you but she'll never let you finish it. She's not going to accept you doing a scene from *Mary, Mary*.'

We went in anyway, and I started my scene and three or four minutes into it she stopped me, and he gave me a look – I told you so. She looked at me and asked whom I had studied with.

'I just got here from Kansas and have mostly studied with my mom.' Again he shot me one of those 'good grief' looks.

Uta Hagen took a drag off her cigarette and said, 'Well, honey, she taught you well. I'd like you to come into my class.' My friend almost fell on his butt. I joined her class, which was a huge honor for anyone, especially someone 'right off the bus.'

I want to preface what I'm going to say next with the acknowledgment that I consider Uta Hagen a brilliant actor, teacher, icon, and an incredibly genuine person. And, yes, her method was not right for me. Unbeknownst to me, I was walking into a classroom which was going to ask me again to substitute my knowingness with an intellectual approach, breaking everything down into beats, figuring everything out, dissecting it and then putting it back together. It didn't take me very long to figure out that when I did it her way, she never liked it. When I did it my instinctive way, she always loved what I did. She'd say, 'That's how it all comes together. You take the time and get your beats, and you thoroughly know your character.' I got it. I had to keep doing what I knew best. I had to keep doing what was right for me.

I shone when I would just become a conduit or channel of my intention. I would come to life with the knowingness that I didn't have to know. While I was blessed to be in Ms Hagen's class, it just reinforced my instinctive approach. Sometimes the Universe teaches you the lesson by taking you in the opposite direction. Uta Hagen's knowingness was not my knowingness. What worked for her didn't work for me. What worked for my mom did work for me. It was this constant search to understand everyone's truth and how that applied to my own. Even the characters that I played begged the question, 'Who am I? How do I find the truthfulness of who I am?' Every intention in my acting and in my life arose from being truthful in the moment. When I stayed in 'the moment of now,' I was secure.

It was freedom when I was there in my truthfulness, and hell when I was in someone else's. It was high creativity when I was there and manipulation when I wasn't. It was me when I was there and it was them when I wasn't. Maybe I didn't resonate with the intellectual formula, but mine was working for me. Or in my career, anyway. Other areas of my life didn't flow as easily, especially relationships. I think it was those confusing male/female role models I was struggling to understand. Maybe I was still trying to take care of men because I failed to take care of my dad. Or maybe, just maybe, it just made me feel safe. Whatever the reason, romantic relationships have always plagued me. I will sometimes give myself up in humiliating ways that don't celebrate and honor me.

And here I was, right off the bus, and in another relationship. He was a good man … smart, creative, and evolved. But I always felt that I was the lesser of the two. We both looked at me as 'the kid from Kansas who didn't know shit.' In discussions, I would surrender my point of view because I hadn't mastered the language of the rebuttal. The trust that kept me in the flow in my career, as well as my wonderful naiveté, seemed to be detrimental in other areas of my life. I was living with someone who I wanted to love me, but I couldn't love myself enough to be loved. It is a challenge that has presented itself often in my life. And as with all things that don't serve us, the resentment mounts, the dam breaks, and we either falter or rise up to learn the lesson.

My boyfriend started berating me one day. 'You're such a Pollyanna! You're always sweet; everything's good …'

It just pushed my button, and I turned around in anger and said, 'But I'm the one who's making money, I'm the one who's working, and I'm the one who's having fun and I'm the one who's in my joy. And if you know so much, then why aren't you doing what I'm doing?'

He was an exceptionally intelligent person, who had a law

degree, and was smart enough to know he had lost that argument. He looked at me. 'I'm sorry. You're right. You're absolutely right.'

I thought, Wow. I spoke up for myself, even with the fear of being judged, and was heard and acknowledged. It certainly changed our relationship. In that instant, it was clear how the yin/yang yo-yo of my mixed life-messages would limit my light if I didn't choose to shine my truth as brightly as I could. I had to claim my light. It's always been that fight for clarity. You can't go for a dream carefully. You can't say to the Universe: Give me this, sort of. It's like a confusing direction from a director! You have to come forward in that clarity, that creativeness – the truthfulness that's you. This is my light – gotta let it shine – and I'm gonna let me shine all the way.

All those years, I was trying to figure out the fear and safety and judgment aspects of intent and how they could coexist with: I know it, I'm fabulous, I'm wonderful, and I'm joyful. When I could stay out of the fear and just know, I could effortlessly carry out my intention. But when the fear of judgment and being safe rushed in, I would always have hills to climb: I wouldn't get the audition or I wouldn't book the job. It was something about my beautiful, wonderful, incredible naiveté that always had the Universe just showing up for me. I trusted life. And I worked hard. I beat the streets and studied and learned and practiced. And I just knew I could do it. I loved to play. I allowed it, and I got it. My intention was to succeed when I got there, and I did. I was able to hold on to what I knew and not buy into the fears and the indoctrination of people who 'knew more.' For me, creation has always been about heart and beingness. Those years helped me understand how to bring my head and heart together: to intellectually figure how to carry out my intention and then move into the heart of creation and let it flow.

I knew from talking to acting friends that film and television were different from theater: more in the moment, quicker, and more intimate. I decided at that point to make my way to Los Angeles. There was a joke going around where an actor from LA and an actor from NY meet in the Midwest and yell at each other: 'Go back, go back – there's no work!' Everybody from NY was going to LA, and everybody from LA was coming to NY. We didn't know that it was really about us, and not the place we were going. We didn't know that 'wherever you go, there you are.' So I used my dance background and booked an industrial show for Koogle peanut butter. As I remember, it was a mixture of peanut butter and chocolate: the two things you could spread all over my body and make me really happy! In fact, the costume was so skimpy I could've used some extra padding. Just picture fluorescent pink tights with big, huge white eyes with black centers that rolled around as we danced. I was a hot-pink Koogle peanut, and I danced my way across America so I could come to LA and hopefully attract film people who weren't so much into the formula and didn't have to break everything down. Maybe film acting would be more suitable for me.

I brought my naive little dancer's body out to LA and called a friend. I had a great commercial agent and he had a great theatrical agent, and we introduced each other to our respective agents and we both got signed. I was off and running. I left NY knowing that I couldn't leave my knowing. I left NY knowing that whatever I did naturally, it worked for me. I had to hold out for that. I had to be safe being me. I couldn't carry out the intentions that I had for myself when I was trying to be someone else. No, I would choose to be the creative, passionate, joyful light of Deanna Lee Bowers, aka Dee Wallace, actor and seeker of truth.

Chapter Two

The Art of Beingness

Deanna Lee Bowers and Dee Wallace had a lot in common, and a lot to bring together. We both knew we wanted to be free, creative, and happy. We both knew we were happiest in the moments when we were authentic. But Dee Wallace had to be in business for herself. And, quite frankly, both were a little perplexed at how to bring the feminine energy of heart and marry the masculine energy of business.

My models from childhood were confusing. My father had feminine energy and didn't fit the role of a male breadwinner, and killed himself because he couldn't hold up his end. While my mother was feminine and creative, she worked a job and was the family's provider. I didn't have clear-cut definitions of male and female roles. Eventually I came to realize that to be in balance I had to combine the feminine and masculine energies, the yin and the yang, which we all have in various combinations. Again the secret for me was being in the moment and allowing both sides to harmoniously work together.

I had learned a lot during those two years at the Berghof Studio: how to break scenes down, rebuild them, let them go; and what worked for me, what didn't work for me, and what I had to hold on to and how easy it was to give it away. Uta left me with a great sense of respect for acting – actually the name of her brilliant book on the subject. She taught me to honor my fellow actors and their process and their passions and fears. She taught me the emotional ride of the actor. But I wasn't with her long enough for her to share any of the secrets of success in the business that I loved so much.

For that, I had come to California. And as usual, my naiveté again served me well. An acquaintance I knew in New York had graciously allowed me to stay with her until I found an apartment. Three days after I arrived, she made it lovingly clear that she would drive me around to look at places. It hadn't occurred to me I'd need a car in LA.

So off we went to look at places, and they were all rather dumpy for what I could afford. But the landlord at the last place suggested I meet his friend who ran an apartment complex on Larrabee off Sunset. It was a central location, and I loved the complex. It was run by a middle-aged bachelor who had a soft spot for beginning actors. My heart sank when he told me the price of this great apartment.

'I'm sorry,' I lamented. 'It's double what I can afford.'

He looked at me, hesitated, and then offered a solution. 'There was a nice young lady here earlier who couldn't afford it either. Maybe you could share.'

We called her, and she came by. We hit it off and moved in together. We were best friends for two years. Gram Bow even made us matching dresses. Very Kansas. Now I needed a car!

It's the God's truth that the next story happened as described. I was eating alone in a restaurant on Sunset the next week. I really couldn't afford it, but the place helped me feel 'okay' about my prospects. In retrospect, I was saving my money 'just in case.' After all, I was starting out anew! So, I'm sitting there looking all virginal and lonely, and this lovely couple sits down at the table next to me. They happen to hear me explain to the waiter, who was flirting shamelessly with me, that I 'just got here from Kansas.' (New York wasn't as good a line!)

They introduced themselves and said they, too, were from Kansas – Kansas City, in fact! Well, we talked story and what do ya know? They knew my mom! They asked me to join them. I told them of the apartment, and how I was searching for a car to replace my Rent-a-Wreck. Well, the man's brother owned a car dealership in LA. He got him on the phone. By the time dessert arrived, I had a loan out on a good used car with no finance charges for six months. I couldn't believe it myself. As I was taking the money out of the savings, I kept saying, 'Relax, Dee. That's what you saved the money for!' I set my sights on the next task at hand. Just being me was working out pretty well.

As you recall, I had already been set up with an agent, and now I needed to get film for a reel, an important tool for the actor. Fate took me to a coffee shop (it seems many of my angels do caffeine) in Beverly Hills. As I was killing time between making the rounds – an actor's term for endlessly dropping off pictures in hopes of actually getting a meeting – I ran into a friend from my acting class in New York. I mentioned that I needed film, and he said that his good friend, Director So-and-So, had just called to see if he knew a really good actress to play the part of a rape victim in *The Streets of San Francisco*. There were only two lines, but it was a big rape scene that opened the episode, and he needed someone really strong who could pull it off. Was I interested? You've gotta be kidding me.

So he called this director and expounded endlessly on how great a dramatic actress I was, how I had knocked them dead in New York, and the director believed him. He called my agent, and I got the part with no audition and no meeting because he was already in San Francisco prepping for the shoot. This was unheard of for an unknown actor. My agent called half an hour later and wanted to know how I pulled this off. I couldn't tell him, 'I'm guided,' so I simply said: 'Good things just happen to me.' And I was blithely off to San Francisco with my naiveté and my knowingness working for me. Didn't this happen to everybody? I thought. When I arrived, I was rushed to wardrobe, rushed to the set, rushed through makeup, and rushed into shooting the scene. This was all a little too fast for me to get into 'my moment.' I had never shot a scene in front of a camera, but I knew the basics and how to hit my mark from theater work. However, getting intimate with more than a prop was new to me.

We hurriedly ran through the staging for the camera; they touched up my makeup, and in the next moment I heard someone call out 'Action.' I did what every actor does when caught off guard. I acted. Badly. I'm sure I sounded like a four-year-old trying to play-act.

'CUUUUUUUUUUUT,' the director yelled out and came running at me with venom in his eyes.

'What the hell was that?' he screamed. 'Robert told me you could act, that you were brilliant. But that was lame. It was awful. It sucked. Can you do this? If not, tell me now and we'll get a replacement. Well?'

A deer caught in headlights. Fear. Major fear crept through my body. Judgment. This was the ultimate judgment for an actor about their creativity. And I was letting everyone down. I felt hot tears of anger and embarrassment running down my cheeks.

'I'm ready now,' I said, my eyes flashing. 'But I need to go back to the beginning.'

The director rolled his eyes, the cameraman cued up, and then, 'Roll, mark, ACTION.' Let me tell you, this was the best rape scene in the history of television. Dee left, and that poor helpless victim appeared and suffered her horrible fate. I was so caught up in the terror of it all that I didn't even hear the director yell 'Cut.' I couldn't come back that quickly from this emotional self, and when I finally reentered my body, everyone on the entire set was just standing there with their mouths open. Shit. Now what? I thought. The director came running over and threw his arms around me, then stepped back and looked me in the eyes.

'Robert was right. You were great. Thank you.' Turning to his gawking crew, he said, 'Okay, what's next?'

My triumph was short-lived, but glorious nevertheless. On the way back to my dressing room, I began to dissect what had happened. Why had I frozen on the set? I needed to figure that out so it would never happen again. I went back in my mind: I had received my script, read and studied it, and then broke down the scene. I thought about the girl and her life and all the things I'd learned in Uta's class, and I ended up using a method that I knew didn't work for me. I had just simply gone into my head and out of my heart, into my intellect and out of my beingness, or my connection to my whole self and the whole of life. Why did I do the very things that I knew didn't serve me? Fear. The obvious answer was staggering: because this was the big time; this was important. It was so important that I had to do it the right way, the important way, the 'head' way – the way that had never worked for me. I regressed back to a place of safety and control, so 'they would be pleased.' But the powers that be weren't happy. What they really wanted to see was 'me.'

When I remained in the power of Dee and stopped trying to please 'them,' my mind stopped working and my natural instincts took over; my energy rocketed up the scale and from there I was somehow able to draw on hidden aspects of myself to create this embodiment. I was in her, and she was in me, and it was simply amazing. I wanted more of this. In this very moment, I wanted more of this beingness in acting and living. But something else got planted in me that day: the belief, if only a small kernel, that I had to suffer for my craft or for what I wanted. The director's wrath had evoked fear in me that ended in acknowledgment and praise. It was the beginning of a side path, an offshoot of wrong interpretations about giving up one's self in some way to be great or to make it work, be it an acting gig or a relationship.

I took these lessons back to Los Angeles and happily told everyone how I had gotten raped on cue very brilliantly; thank you for the applause, but I was ready for my next challenge. My agent was quite impressed, although he didn't have any ready work for me. But never one to rest on my laurels, I set out to make more contacts. It was almost impossible back then to get onto the studio lots to meet casting directors and producers. Actors would have group meetings to come up with elaborate schemes to meet these people. I, of course, knew nothing of such roadblocks and joyously set out to do what you do in Kansas to meet someone: you bake cookies. Chocolate chip was my favorite, and I baked twelve dozen. I wrapped them in pretty little baskets, tied them with even prettier little bows, and off I went to Universal Studios. I just showed up at the gate with baskets of cookies for delivery, batted those eyes innocently, and the guard let me inside without a question. While I was dropping them off, my knowingness – or some would say synchronicity – created a brilliant opportunity. Reuben Cannon, a very well-respected casting director, happened to step out of his inner sanctum as I was dropping off a basket of cookies with my photo and acting sheet. He invited me in for a short chat. Chocolate chip was his favorite, too.

I again used the line that I had just arrived from Kansas (always a statement that somehow really engaged people), and as we were chatting and munching on cookies, a call came in from the soundstage. 'Oh no,' I heard him say. And then the most miraculous (or natural, depending on your perspective) thing happened.

He looked at me and said, 'What size do you wear?'

Without hesitation I replied, 'What size do you need?'

It seems the actress in a television drama, who was supposed to rescue the star having a heart attack in her restaurant, had called in sick. Too bad for her. I stuffed myself into that size six cocktail outfit and went down to the soundstage. I had learned my lessons well from *The Streets of San Francisco*, and was determined to not repeat the same mistakes. I waited to get to the set and run through the rehearsal before I thought about how to play the scene. It worked! I was perfectly in the moment during the first take. But then the director approached me, as I waited anxiously.

'We have a slight problem,' he whispered. I could feel the fear of a judgment rise in me, flashbacks from that previous gig.

22

'You're doing a beautiful job' – but, but, but is all I could hear in expectation – 'but Mr. So-and-So asked that you not touch him.' I did a double take: Excuse me? The guy is having a heart attack, and how am I supposed to help him if I can't touch him? What about all those 'real moments' that had just happened; what about my organic acting beingness? 'He's the star and you're a day player. Find a way to make it work.'

I didn't like this turnabout. This job wasn't fun anymore. But that good Kansas work ethic kicked in; I had a job to do, and I didn't want to let Mr Cannon down. So I took the next organic approach to the scene that was real for me. I freaked out, or the character did. If I couldn't be smart and rescue him by loosening his tie, holding his head, etc., then I would be the dumb, flustered, inept waitress that went into sheer panic: the dumb blonde. And it worked! The director loved it; Mr Untouchable was content, and my agents called once again and said, 'How did you do this?' Life in Los Angeles was good; I was studying on the job, getting lessons you could never learn in a classroom – like how not to be real because you are a day player. That was a real eye opener. I was also getting lessons in humility.

My commercial agent called me into her office. 'You're fat,' she said flatly. 'You've gained 20 pounds since we signed you. You're not booking as much. Lose it.' I did. In three weeks I was back to my actor's weight. Talk about tough love. Alas, I was booking commercials but not film jobs. I soon discovered that I didn't get the same respect that a studying actor commands. True, my two years with Uta Hagen did punch up my resumé. But ultimately, you were more respected as a 'serious' actor when you were consistently studying. I set about collecting names of acting coaches.

There were five people that kept surfacing over and over, and so I audited them. Four of them were very classically oriented, didn't use film scripts, worked on the same scene for weeks, and basically taught the Method of breaking down scenes, studying intentions (which basically came down to 'What does she want?'), creating beats – very heady approaches. I already knew that didn't work for me. I ended up at Jeff Corey's class. I adored Jeff. We did interesting, off-the-wall exercises that were more in the moment. We did do scene work and practice outside of class with our scene partner, but they were film scenes, or stage material that adapted itself more readily to film. I lived for the times we got to work in front of the camera. I loved not having to project to the audience, to be real and small and intimate and emotionally powerful internally. I learned a lot in that class. It reaffirmed my approach that the head could be invited into the scene, and then asked to leave so the character could channel through me. But I must admit, it was hit and miss in class. Sometimes I was there in the moment brilliantly, and sometimes I couldn't get there because I was watching to see if I brought what I had rehearsed. And I couldn't quite figure out how to take everything I learned in class into the few auditions I was getting. I was moving a little too much into my head, and because of that, a little too slowly up the ladder of success.

During this period, Gram Bow became quite ill with appendicitis. Mom informed me, 'They thought it was best to put her directly into a home for the elderly,' instead of taking her back to her home. I felt bad and recalled a touching conversation I had with her my senior year of high school.

Gram had taken me aside and said, 'DD, I want you to promise me something. You're the only one I trust. Don't let them put me in a home unless there's just no other way.' Yes. Gram needed me. I flew back and tactfully intervened. I hired a wonderful African-American caregiver named Lil. Gram loved her immediately, and the feeling was mutual. Lil was a Godsend and lived with her until Gram made her transition years later. It felt good to honor this woman who had always been there for me.

While I was there, I was able to question Mom on the actor's dilemma of being consistent in one's performances. How could she give those readings over and over and make it new each time? Was there some secret?

'I don't know, DD,' she pondered. 'I don't get to do it often enough, and I'm so happy when I do get the chance, that the same reading becomes great fun every time.' A light went on. Holy Heck, I thought. Acting was becoming a real job for me; it was becoming my provider of rent, food, and clothes, not my passion, not my sacred calling. I asked Mom the secret of balancing the two, but of course that had been her lifelong struggle as well, and she had no answers. It looked like I had to pull off this magical balancing act for both of us. It occurred to me that I didn't really consider commercial bookings as acting, so I didn't have any pressure to perform, to 'be good,' to 'do it right.' I just went in, stayed in the moment, and had a good time. And, of course, I was very successful. I wasn't taking that approach in my serious acting. I was starting to try too hard, and to figure it all out ahead of time. This made me go into fear about choosing incorrectly, and that shut down the channel to my whole self, or my beingness. It became my watchingness instead. What was going to happen? When? How well? How much? That long-buried concern for my safety was creeping back into my work. It was time to move on from here. I reminded myself: your mind can only take you so far. Then you have to just Be.

Again I put my 'intention' feelers out into the Universe. There must be someone who understands this way of working, I said to myself. This is a film town after all, and acting real in the moment is every actor's motto. You guessed it. A week later I was, yes, getting coffee when I ran into an acquaintance. I was lamenting my plight when he stopped me mid-sentence: 'I have the place. I just joined it. The Charles Conrad Studio. He only lets you read the scene once and tells you not to think about it.' My energy literally leapt out of my body. I knew. I knew even before I audited it that I was home. I immediately called the studio from the nearest pay phone. I had my appointment for the next week and my meeting with Conrad after that.

When I arrived and sat down across from him, Charles looked at me and asked why I wanted to join his studio. I said, 'Because I want acting to be fun and joyful and in the moment.'

He took one beat, smiled, and said, 'You're in, kid.'

And I was in for the ride of my life – and my career. We began each class with some kind of lesson on energy or spiritual philosophy or conscious creation. We were allowed to read the scene only once – preferably without emotion – to just get the information and move on and trust. The object was to get your energy extremely high (his whole technique was largely based on this approach) and connect by throwing your energy to the other actor, and then receive theirs, and lobby it back and forth. DON'T PLAN. TRUST. Make it Authentic! Could it be? Had I really been led to an acting coach that forced you to just Be? You had little time or information to not Be: to mess around with figuring out how to stay safe by knowing too much. It not only opened up my world of acting, but it was my introduction to the world of true spirituality. I could be one with everything in the moment. I was free, and just trusted it to happen. This process took away all my fear. How could you get it wrong if there weren't any decisions to make? Consciousness became acting, and acting became consciousness. Acting was born consciously in Charles Conrad's class as a spiritual path for me. Some people find this flow in sales, some in teaching, and some in parenting. It is the flow of conscious knowing and trust.

I saw unbelievable performances in that class. People acted out having seizures when they had never experienced them, would limp through scenes as crippled characters when the part required it but the script didn't specify it. Actors would know the subtext of what was happening in the whole piece even when there was no mention of it in their scene. Sometimes the intensity of the connection in that class was so overwhelming we would sit there, breathlessly moved by the sheer truthfulness of the acting.

It even transcended acting. It was life. And that, of course, made it painfully clear when anyone did not trust the process, held on to the need to control, and were in fear that the net wouldn't be there. Then the performances were 'fine' but predictable; competent, but not magical. Like a life lived without passion and spontaneity: the days are handled but the years are mediocre.

Charles spent much of his creative time retraining good 'method actors' from the habits they had come to rely on. 'It doesn't make sense to have this emotion with this line,' they would lament. But every time they trusted the process and committed themselves, it did make sense – in its own unique and wondrous way. Just like my naive knowing, when you really trusted, the net appeared – as a friend in a coffee shop, a part in a casting director's office, and an acting class that was teaching cutting-edge techniques. I didn't and couldn't have planned any of those remarkable coincidences. But my beingness opened the door for creation to happen. And it did.

I was gloriously home in every sense of the word.

And my clear intention of joyfully working and living this way and creating a career of passion was already manifesting more than I could imagine. Being dropped by my agent was a part of that plan. It threw me into a brief panic. Just as everything was going so smoothly, I found myself without representation – this was equated to no livelihood. It never occurred to me that lots of actors got work without agents. I just couldn't think out of the box. I thought that my agents hadn't been doing their job anyway – I needed to get out for bigger roles in bigger movies. And, of course, the Universe gives you what you ask for, and sometimes it comes in scary ways. Now what? I knew that I needed a bigger agent and so I threw out the intention net. My first thought was to hang out all day at the local coffee shop and see what turned up.

Around that time Charles decided to mount a scene-night, and invited several casting directors, agents, and producers to watch his students perform. There were approximately twelve scenes mounted by the top actors in the studio, and I was one of them. My scene was an amazing emotional roller coaster – my forte. At the end of that night, I was offered an audition for the lead in a religious film. I auditioned and got the part. It was a strong character: a battered wife of an alcoholic. As in life so in art: I had 'knowledge' of alcoholism and its effects. I traveled to Des Moines, Iowa to work on the film for four weeks in the sweltering heat for a man who would end up becoming a lifelong friend, Don Thompson. I find it interesting that God and spirituality was again weaving itself through my fledgling career. Don not only directed but also nurtured me, prayed with and counseled me, and encouraged me to be who I was. It was an amazing experience of solidifying my technique, seeing how well it worked given the space, and how I could unconditionally trust it. Looking back now, I wish I had been aware of how my acting approach was a metaphor for my life: trust, allow, and be. I just wasn't quite conscious enough back then to understand that yet.

When the film was finished and viewed, it was clear that I had given a powerful performance, or a heart performance you could viscerally feel, which is what Charles taught me. I decided to ask Don, in all my naiveté, if he could schlep the film cans out to Los Angeles so I could invite agents to attend a screening. I desperately needed representation. He graciously agreed. I carefully put together a short list of agents that were my best bets and invited them. When I told friends and colleagues of my plan, they were aghast. 'They'll laugh you out of the room. You can't show a religious film to Hollywood agents!' Echoes of the Uta Hagen audition danced through my head. But I figured that if they couldn't see my performance for what it was, I didn't want to be represented by them anyway. At the end of the screening, nine out of the ten agencies wanted me. Again, my simple knowing saved me and propelled me forward in my career: a barrage of films and television work.

I immediately booked the lead in *The Hills Have Eyes*, and was thrown into working with several actors who 'planned everything.' I would rehearse with them but only up to the point where I could still be true to the technique. I wanted them to be as good as they could be, but I knew what served me. There were, however, some frustrating moments when I simply had to say, 'Sorry. I can't do that until the take.'

I had plenty of practice harmonizing these different approaches throughout my marriage to Christopher Stone. Poor Chris. He worked on his parts, made notes, did background work on his characters. It worked for him; he was a wonderful actor. We would often joke that he was living with his leading lady, but he couldn't even rehearse! I remember walking onto the set of *The Howling*, and we had a big fight scene. Our director Joe Dante asked us how we planned to play the scene.

Chris smirked, 'I know how I'm gonna play it. I don't have a clue about my co-star.'

Joe blinked. 'Didn't you guys work on it last night?'

This drew another smirk. 'My leading lady doesn't rehearse.'

Joe shook his head; we played the scene brilliantly, and he never asked us again. We had a very long string of successful films working with these opposite techniques. The point is: Chris trusted his, I trusted mine, and we both respected the other's. His was the masculine approach of knowing from control; mine was the feminine approach of knowing from instinct or feeling. The creation was always beautiful.

This was interesting: how positively the directors responded, once they saw how the technique worked. My opening line on the first day of shooting was to assure them I wanted to give them what they needed, but asked if they could trust me, watch the dailies, and then we'd go from there. There was very little discussion about my technique after the first day. They especially loved how quickly I worked with this 'in the moment' approach. I liked to shoot the rehearsal and get it down on the first take if possible. It was new and fresh! This saved so much time and film. Everybody won. And I could live in the moments of my character's life. Sure, there were some movie people along the way that questioned it – at least at first. For instance, I had developed the habit of doing deep knee bends, shaking my hands, and then taking some deep breaths before each scene. Actors do weird things, and that was my ritual.

I was working on *Hart to Hart,* and the first day on the set Robert Wagner looked at my warm-up routine and laughed. 'What the hell?' he asked. The second day he walked in and smiled, shook his head, and turned around and walked off. After watching me act in some very intense scenes, at the end of that second day he approached me, smiled and said, 'How exactly does that work?' As they say, if it works, leave it alone.

I have learned that I like it authentic, easy and joyful. Overworking prevents the flow from happening. When I used my mind to set the intention and then let instinct create the creative flow, my ego didn't put me in fear and create self-judgments. We all came in with that feminine instinctual knowing. I had it secured in my acting. But could I hold on to it in my life?

Chapter Three

The High-Energy Zone

As I look back on those years at the Conrad Studio, it was like *Camelot*: the beginning of a new era in my life, and in the art of acting as a metaphor for living life from the heart. It was there that I learned a technique that solidified my natural approach to acting, and would hold me steady in the midst of laborious rehearsals, method actors, angry directors, egotistical producers, some uneducated casting directors, and my own fears. It was my compass in the storm, the yellow brick road that always took me back to Oz.

I knew there was gold at the end of this road, and like E.T. I was making my way to the 'home' of me. But the travel was often laborious and frustrating. There were months of auditioning with no real bookings and therefore no income. I tried a brief stint at waitressing, but in a town full of professional actor/waiters I was outmatched. I used my teaching degree to do some private tutoring, and I taught several classes at a wonderful dance studio, including a class on musical comedy. We had a great time performing funny renditions of everything from 'One Singular Sensation' from *A Chorus Line* to 'You've Got to Pick a Pocket or Two' from *Oliver!* I still knew that I was going to make it, but the financial strain of getting there was exhausting. The Conrad Studio was my salvation, and I was more than willing to eat peanut butter sandwiches to pay for it.

One of the most important dictums of the Conrad Process was discipline. Charles was big on discipline. You had to be there fifteen minutes before class was scheduled to start: pick up your scene at check-in, handle any payment issues, and read your scene to move into the focused energy that you were to bring to the reading. If you were late and didn't call, you didn't work that class. And you got reamed royally. Those may sound like very simple rules, but it was amazing how many people fought them. Some of the students felt like they were 'being treated like children,' and not allowed to handle this preparation as their responsibility. They would arrive in the nick of time, prepare their scene while others were working, and be late enough with payments to create disharmony with the assistant. At first, none of us realized that the lessons started before you even arrived at class. It wasn't until I was well into studying with Charles that I grasped that maintaining discipline and that being punctual was an intricate part of his entire acting technique. If you were too scattered or undisciplined to be on time, how could you then be in the moment for your performance here or on the set? And as in life, you have to 'show up.' Preferably on time, because 'God helps those who help themselves.' I never really absorbed the meaning of that saying until it was presented from an energy standpoint. If you don't hold the intention and belief, it's impossible for the manifestation to follow. So show up, shut up, and do the work!

I had never had any spiritual training. I had grown up in a religious family and received instruction, but it never occurred to me that there was a difference. I had heard the word 'Buddhist,' but I had never been exposed to their beliefs or met any Buddhists in the good old Kansas City of that era. If my family had interacted with any Jewish people, it was a cold day in hell. So I had no way of connecting discipline practices with spirituality as it is found in these religions. I did, however, know about discipline. I had been a dancer for years and studied with a prima ballerina from Germany. Oh yes, I knew a lot about discipline. But it wasn't until I was required to read *Zen in the Art of Archery* that I began to understand Charles' general approach to acting as a discipline. That book resonated with who I was, what I had always known, and how I had always lived. Being from Kansas,

I just didn't know that some ancient traditions had created systems of thought around the concept of beingness. Wow. I was a Methodist practicing Buddhism and didn't even know it! My approach was totally unconscious and haphazard, but I knew it because it came naturally to me. The task, here and in life, was to find a consistent approach – a standard to apply in all cases.

And it was painfully clear in class when any of the students were fighting this approach. *Zen in the Art of Archery* was about the journey of a novice archer from the West learning how to shoot a bow from the Zen way of thinking, which meant no thinking at all. For months, the teacher made the young man just hold the bow, then the arrow, and then the bow and the arrow together. For months, he wasn't allowed to shoot the arrow. 'Be at one with the bow,' the master would instruct him. Don't think about your equipment. Don't think about hitting the target. Don't think about the intention. Just become one with the tools. This approach to acting was an enormous challenge for actors who had come from the method school of acting and university programs. They had been taught to break everything down and to think, think, think about what the material meant and what the subtext was and how to bring it to life. Finding the acting beats was where everything started and ended. For them, Charles' method of not thinking the scene through was like soldiers walking across a field in a foreign land with buried mines and snipers. What you didn't know wasn't safe, and so many clung to what they knew: the Method. And that was a death knell with the Conrad Technique.

One of the key precepts was being able to raise your energy from the mental level to the high-energy zone where you connected to the greater whole and its life energies – it's where the flow happens. I fondly remember a student, who eventually became a good friend, who struggled with this approach right from the start. Class was set up with four rows of chairs, each row a bit higher for maximum viewing. Charles sat in the middle of the front row, and everyone knew not to sit behind or beside him because any movement could break his focus and put him through the roof. There were two chairs and a table in front of him about three feet away, and the lights would highlight the actors. It was all terribly dramatic, but nothing compared to what actually happened on stage.

So that night my friend made his way to the table and sat down next to his partner, picked up the scene, and dove right into it. Before he even got a word out, Charles stopped him. 'What are you doing?'

'What do you mean?' the actor asked.

'What are you doing?' Charles asked again impatiently.

'I'm … I'm … I'm beginning the scene.'

'How?' he asked.

'I'm … getting ready to tell her goodbye.'

'How do you know that?' Charles asked.

'What?'

'How do you know that?' Charles asked in a louder voice, becoming more excited. I saw my friend freeze.

'Because I read the scene …' he said in exasperation.

'NOOOOOOOO,' he shouted. Charles looked like he was going to physically attack him. 'You fucking know that because your energy is so high that it has taken you out of your fucking head and you are living in that moment!' He paused for a second. 'And don't start again without your energy high.'

We had all stopped breathing and had put ourselves in that hot seat. My friend tried to regain his composure and begin: his energy was sure as hell up there now! He took a deep breath. What happened next stunned us all. His partner reached over and slapped him hard. He broke down into tears, and then looked up. He told her that he was leaving her with such pathos that it stopped her cold. It was 'fucking' perfect. Perfect and beautiful and absolutely stunning. Not in a million years could your intellectual mind have figured how to play that beat in that way.

The scene ended. The class applauded. And then the guy stood up, glared at Charles, and angrily exclaimed, 'I'm outta here. This is bullshit. And it's not for me.'

No, I thought. This approach is not for weak souls, and only for authentic explorers of their own truth. As in life, we often get slapped silly until we realize how inauthentic we are 'acting.' I ruminated that night over my friend's departure, and a huge sadness arose in me; I realized that in many ways this was how my father would have handled the situation. He was a delicate soul with a creative spirit, and his wartime experience had damaged his tender heart. Like my friend who couldn't take the 'heat' and bailed out of class, Daddy bailed out of life with alcohol as his escape. Mom tried to save him – the whole family tried – but to no avail. Today they would call it post-traumatic stress syndrome, but back then they only treated the alcoholism, not the cause. And I was determined to be strong and deal with my wounds; I wasn't going to bail out of acting or life.

My naiveté and knowingness, coupled with my dance discipline, united in an agreement with my soul to follow this guru to the letter and do exactly what he asked of me. And the longer I was in the Studio, the more I realized that Charles was just that: my guru. He wasn't simply teaching me how to act; he was teaching me how to live life from the center outward. It was the discipline of beingness as an equation that I could depend on in every situation. Life and art meshed into one beautiful dance of understanding.

I can remember dutifully arriving on that first day of class after I was added to the roster. I picked up my scene, read it once, and sat down square in the middle so I could see both people equally. When I felt I was ready, I walked to the front and my partner for that day followed after me. I don't know why, but I went to the corner, did some deep knee bends, shook my hands, took a deep breath, and came back to the chairs to start the scene. I vividly remember this little regimen, because I have done it prior to every scene in every project ever since.

We had been briefed in the Conrad Process, and I sat down to focus on my partner. The next thing I knew, I couldn't find my lines in the script. They just seemed to be jumping all over the page. I was feeling humiliated. I was a better actress than this! I began to panic, and looked down on the page for safety.

'Get off the page. Connect!' I heard Charles yell. I tried to look up. I tried, but I lost the lines again, and went back down to the page. I felt that old fear of judgment creeping into me. I panicked again. 'Get off the page, Dee!' he yelled again, more impatiently. Gee, I thought, it's my first class. Give a girl a break. The scene ended, and so did my composure. I took a breath and my tears flowed.

'Why are you crying?' Charles asked.

'Because I feel humiliated. I can act better than this,' I said.

'Ah,' replied the master, 'but you haven't learned … to just be with it.' He proceeded to explain that concept using the metaphor of a dancer expecting to do five pirouettes her first day in class. He knew I was a dancer. It was smart teaching. 'Would you expect to perfectly perform five turns your first dance class?' he inquired.

'Of course not,' I answered.

'Then will you trust me to teach you a whole new way to act, using a blank page of knowing nothing?'

'Yes,' I said. It didn't escape me that I had already decided to do just that. From the moment I walked into class, I was determined to play by the rules, to follow the technique to the letter. But without knowing it consciously, the fear of being bad and looking foolish took me back into a control space, and then I was bad. Very bad.

Charles then gave me an exercise on how to practice sight-reading and I did it for a couple weeks. I was told to read anything – magazines, newspapers, scripts – and to connect with myself in the mirror while picking up more and more lines at a time. It was a technical discipline that would lay the groundwork for the art. I was getting to know the bow.

After that first class I wanted to understand why I had not been able to find the words on the script page during that reading.

'You were caught between two worlds,' he replied mysteriously.

'Excuse me?' I inquired, giving him a skeptical look. Was this some far-out metaphysical explanation? Well, yes and no. On one level, as he explained, I was stuck because of how I had studied scripts in the past and this begged the question: how the hell can you know the words if you haven't looked at them? It wasn't in my belief system that I could do that. On the other hand, I was halfway to knowing that I created everything. I just couldn't trust it because my mind kept me in the realm of probable outcomes and not the upper reaches of what was possible.

'How do I resolve that split?' I implored.

'Energy,' he replied. 'High, focused, unknowing energy.' I began to pursue another question when Charles interrupted me. 'Go home, Dee. It's only the first class.'

But, like always, I wanted it THEN. My mother and first acting coach remembered my impatience very well. I had shared with her my excitement about this new class and how I wanted to learn everything immediately, and that I wished I could just lock Charles in a room and pick his brain. Three days later I received a greeting card from her: on the cover were two vultures sitting on a telephone wire, with one of them looking angrily at his partner. I opened it and the print in bold letters said: 'Patience my ass. I want to kill something NOW.' Underneath in Mom's very neat handwriting were the words: 'Don't kill the process, Deanna. The process is the answer.' Yeah, right, I thought back then. If I had only known, it would have made the climb a lot easier for me. I am afraid that my anxious need to know was partly fueled by the fear of being bad again and being judged for it. I didn't like that feeling. But letting go of outcomes and expectations is paramount for anyone who's creative. As I would later learn from Jody Foster, you have to be willing to be bad to be brilliant. You can't move into your knowingness while you are in fear. Especially in life.

All of Charles' classes began with a spiritual or philosophical exploration, which was inspired by some great magazine article or nugget of truth he had stumbled on during the week in his eternal quest for understanding the human psyche. At my second class, he brought in a number of readings about energy. My ego would have liked to believe they were especially for me, relating to the discussion we had shared the previous week. After you knew Charles, you came to realize that was not the case. He lived in the moment as he taught you to act in the moment. That conversation had probably evaporated into one of the many spiritual dimensions he inhabited. But those particular readings on energy opened an old, familiar door of truth that had been quietly closed since my childhood.

Energy. Everything is energy. Everything is created from energy. And a high vibration of energy creates the best results in any endeavor. He would read us stories from interviews with The Beatles, or cite amazing facts about Michelangelo and a slew of great artists and scientists on the art of managing energy and how they used, directed, and channeled its flow. Always, always the objective was to stir the instincts more than the intellectual mind. He awed me with stories about Einstein and his use of daydreaming and imagination to channel some of his greatest works. The dream world gave us great songs and scientific insights. I loved this exploration. This was so me. This is what I'd known on some level all along but had never articulated. Why hadn't anyone presented this kind of information in college? I was an English and education major. Why hadn't I learned this approach to the creative process? This was why I hated doing lesson plans. This is why I often couldn't write my theme papers until the night before they were due. I was actually coming to understand ME from this acting class.

Energy. Get it high. Really high. Higher than you believe you need to go. Relax your body and let it flow. High energy in a relaxed body, and just let it flow. I was tentative for a while, but at a class early on I felt ready and didn't get up to read until the end. Fear for the first month had made me cautious. I finally felt ready. I walked to the front and immediately went to my corner and did deep knee bends, shook my hands, took a deep breath, and smiled. Oh my God, I thought – that is why I do deep knee bends: to help get the energy high; then I shake my hands to loosen up; and the deep breathing is to relax my body. I walked over to the table, put the script down, and started.

When I finished my scene, I actually felt me coming back into my body. Dee hadn't been there since I sat down in the chair. Dee had left and let the character come in and be in her in the scene. What I had done unconsciously in *The Streets of San Francisco* I had learned to do consciously now! I turned and looked at Charles. He had his hands clasped up around his chin, a huge smile on his face, and little tiny tears in his eyes. We connected. I looked at him, welled up, and whispered, 'Thank you.'

He smiled. 'You know why you're doing better now?' he queried.

'I practice in the mirror every day,' I answered, hoping for a gold star on my scene chart.

'Energy,' he replied, and motioned for the next actor to come up.

I could read from his body language that there would be no discussion. Not today. Today I had made a breakthrough, and he didn't want to intellectualize it. You couldn't really, anyway. It was an experience, as are all good moments in life. The smile got added after that class. I think that was the self-acknowledgement of knowing that I already knew. I was home. I was beginning to understand the spiritual energy of acting, and that it arose from the same center that had always fed my life.

So, I was to learn about the bow: how to raise my energy, keep it on hold, use it, release it, breathe through it, and make it my best friend. I began working out more so I could have more of it. I would power-walk with my dog and bow down to *The Jane Fonda Workout* tape every other day. Some of the students from class would attend lectures on energy at UCLA and try meditation and yoga. I was a dancer and was knowledgeable about breathing and focus when creating dance. But I realized that I depended on action to raise my energy, and I didn't have that crutch in many acting scenes. I read everything I could about energy so I could understand and embrace my new friend. In class we didn't judge anything. We were encouraged to writhe and cry and laugh and fall on the floor. As long as we did it with high energy, our job was simply to study the bow of our instrument and the arrow of energy that was being shot forth from it.

We were in the business of training ourselves to be out of our minds and into our hearts. And in the process, we were shifting our consciousness. We weren't acting; we were exploring being. We were transcending the material and the art. We were transcending our own limitations. We were acting with Spirit and being directed by our higher selves that knew everything. It was amazing. It was a natural narcotic. And you wanted that high all the time.

And all of it seemed to be born in this energy place that Charles talked about incessantly. He would speak about this place where the energy took you into another realm of vibration, where your mind couldn't keep you in fear or control. I had been a very physical being all my life: dancer, gymnast, cheerleader, and runner. Early on I told Charles that I understood energy and had worked with it all my life.

'I'm not talking about physical energy, Dee. I'm talking about vibrational energy: the energy that rises within you from a still place. It's the energy that you are, not that you create.'

'Like Kundalini,' someone in class suggested.

'It even surpasses that,' Charles replied.

I was still baffled; my mind still wanted an explanation. Okay. I didn't know what Kundalini energy was, but it sounded like a good starting point. I had since moved to a tiny studio apartment in San Fernando Valley. It was cheaper and closer to many of the film studios, and to the Conrad Studio. So, one Saturday I put on my sweats and old tennis shoes and power-walked over to the Barnes & Noble, pulled books off the shelves, cuddled up in a big comfy chair, and read for four hours about Kundalini energy. 'My God!' my little Kansas brain exclaimed. 'It's sexual.' Well, when my energy was high and I was channeling the character, it FELT sexual. After a great scene, I used to laughingly quip, 'That was better than sex.' And, quite honestly, I was a pretty sexual person. I liked that feeling. I liked the ride. As I sat there, I half-expected one of my caffeine angels to show up and take me to a Kundalini for Beginners class. Okay. I had done my good-girl homework.

I had it now. So I danced into class that next week ready to share my realization about sex, energy, and acting. When I finished my scene, which felt absolutely brilliant, I looked to Charles. He was just staring at me, but with a look I couldn't decipher.

'What idea did you come in with?' he asked quietly. I sat there and searched myself. I didn't have a clue. 'What did you do to fuck with your energy?'

'I ... I ...' I stammered.

'You looked like you were going to fuck the guy's brains out right there on the table.'

I was embarrassed. 'Well, I just did some research.' I explained to him how his perfect little student went to the perfect little bookstore and dutifully read the perfect little books on Kundalini energy so she could know more about his technique.

'WHAT?' the master roared. 'I never said it was Kundalini!' I reminded him of how someone in class had made that comparison and he didn't dispute it. He looked at me as if I had been banished to actors' hell. 'Dee,' he said with a condescending shake of his head, 'you're like a magnet that picks up everything, but you're picking up junk with the precious metals. Please do me a favor. Don't go studying anything. Just get it.'

I wasn't about to be let off that easily. I could feel me engaging. 'Then tell me now so I get it. I don't want to keep guessing.'

Charles took one of those big breaths that alerted you to get ready for a big pronouncement. 'It's when you see a sunset and you tear up at its grandeur. Or when you make love and lose yourself, or when a mother lactates at the sound of her baby's cry. It's when your greater beingness takes precedence over who you think you are or try to be. It's you being swept away by the essence of who you really are. And yes, that feels like sexual energy or a sexual vibe between people. But it is more, much more than that. It's everything that you are in every dimension of your greater being.' We all waited. He was done. With the chance my 'essence' would be pounced on again, I meekly asked if there were exercises that would help us train and direct this energy.

'Get up,' he commanded. We all stood up. 'Take your hands. Start at your feet and sweep up your body and go over your head. Again. Again. Now hold your palms up. Can you feel the energy?' Feel it? I almost rose up off the floor. 'You just raised the energy physically by directing the aura of energy that extends out from you. And you can do it mentally by visualizing yourself going through this process, and that opens the channel for you to experience your Beingness, your higher self, your authentic self …' Jeez, I thought. Doing this could look a little weird in an audition. We all sat down. 'And now, for Dee's sake, I will explain what the aura is …' Go ahead, I thought. Humiliate me. But I got what I wanted to know.

I practiced night and day with my energy, bringing it up and taking it down. I strived endlessly to 'be my essence.' It was frustrating. Finally, after three weeks of getting NO feedback or comments after my scenes, I'd had it. 'Well,' I demanded, 'am I doing it?'

'No,' came the ominous pronouncement. That was it. I regurgitated volumes of despair and frustration. I flailed, I cried, I screamed. 'Now you're doing it!' Charles yelled excitedly.

'What? What am I doing that's different?' I pleaded.

'Not fucking trying. Just Being.' For some strange reason, in that moment I got the blinding obvious: the high energy forced you to stop trying and allowed you to be it – the essence of yourself. It invited you to be the energy of life. Another breakthrough. How I loved this man.

Slowly I began to realize the subtle brilliance of how everything in class supported the understanding of how to manage our energy by freeing it. The fact that Charles didn't even have an order list but had the actors come up to work when we were ready supported us in learning about our energetic internal pace and peak. It was hell sitting there; your energy could go through the roof if you didn't hold it back. Wanting to act and not act at the same time: being ready and being in fear, being in excited anticipation while unable to take action. We learned to feel when we were ready, to identify our energetic patterns, to be able to harness our energy in such a way that we could keep it 'in the wings' and raise it to perform when we were ready. All this proved invaluable when working on a set for fifteen hours and having to pace yourself to do high-energy scenes with hours between takes. It also served to pace our lives and hold a balance while we were becoming working actors. Again, we were learning the bow, and it was us. We became one with ourselves. And we loved him for that: for giving us ourselves.

Everything flowed from then on. My knowingness and naiveté matched this technique of trust and flow, of allowing things to unfold. I had known this in my life, and the technique affirmed the validity of this approach. Now I had a way to codify and understand it. I had a formula for success in acting and life: intention, energy, direction, relaxation, and flow. I understood it metaphysically so I could choose it consciously. And it helped me feel safer. When I left my mind, it took my fear away. My ego couldn't freak out and yell 'Protect Dee!' That fear of safety and judgment somehow got placed on hold, and my instinctual creative knowingness took over. Yes, Mom, the process was beautiful; it really worked.

Everything in my acting career was happening so fast now. I began booking guest-star roles on television series, and doing tons of commercials. In three short years I had created a successful, stable career. Over and over again, I would hear other actors: 'How did you do it?' 'You got here so fast.' 'Boy, you didn't have to work very hard.' Subtle judgments were flying at me from struggling colleagues who were 'thinking' their way through acting and life. But I had worked hard. I had studied and beat the streets and done numerous commercials pitching coffee, toothpaste, hair coloring, and cooking oil. If you've heard that the biggest film directors in Hollywood are anal, you haven't met the commercial directors – and their clients. I remember with some dismay the anguishing challenge of looking like I really liked a new decaffeinated coffee in one particular commercial. There were seven clients, and after each take the director, producer and their clients would all sit down with their various little egos that had to appear to be earning their money. I would then be hit with a barrage of confusing and conflicting information similar to the hilarious scenes in *Lost in Translation* with Bill Murray. 'More intensity,' indeed, even if it's decaffeinated?

I did various guest-star roles. Most of them were serial dramas like *Police Woman*, *Starsky and Hutch*, *Hotel*, etc. But one of my favorite roles was a has-been actress in an episode of *Taxi* with Judd Hirsch. I adored that man, and he helped me through a very difficult week. I had never done a sitcom. I didn't realize that they keep rewriting it all week – taking things out, trying new lines. I was a basket case! Here I was, studying a technique that taught me to never expect anything, and I was literally crashing with each new rewrite! I called Charles.

'God, Dee. Settle down. Just treat every day as if you had never seen the script and go with what they give you. You can't freak out when you don't know what's coming, just like in real life.' He was right, of course. And Charles just loved for me to bring my stories into class, because everyone could learn about really working on a live set.

Not everyone felt that way, from my fearful perspective. While nothing was really said, I felt that some of my classmates thought I was throwing my success in their faces. I know it was my own projection, because at some level I had trouble accepting it myself. Who was Deanna Bowers from Kansas and why would she have the right to be successful? And so it happened before I even knew it: that subconscious, fearful genetic predisposition reared its nasty head again. I became the little girl in the back seat of my mother's car after celebrating how good I was. That's not okay. I'd better dim that light a little. And so I began judging my own success.

Chapter Four

Judgment Day

I walked in wearing my new silk blouse. That was the 'in thing' to wear at the time: silk blouses. Up-and-coming actresses were drinking coffee in cafés wearing their silk blouses and designer jeans and talking about the parts they were going to get. It became my uniform. The big decision every morning was what fabulous silk blouse in which amazing color was I going to wear that day. It was a safe choice, and I wanted to look great for class. It made me feel more like a professional actor, especially since I was becoming one of the Studio's big success stories. There were many in my class who rose to the top of our profession: Suzanne Somers, Carl Weathers, Steve Eastin, and Veronica Hamel. And that was just from my class. We were the crème de la crème, as it were – not that it meant anything to Charles. He just wanted to see the work. But I secretly believed I was his favorite, the one who played by the rules. He liked that.

So here I was in class, in my purple silk blouse and very tight jeans, ones that I had to lie down on the floor to zip up. And it was my turn to read. I felt the rush of energy and excitement flooding my body. My heart picked up its pace; I took deep breaths to stay focused. It was better than sex. Well, almost as good. I crossed the floor, went to my corner, and did my deep knee bends. Then I heard Charles replacing my customary partner with someone relatively new, who didn't even know the bloody technique. In a nanosecond, I was pissed off and deflated. I began my protest but was interrupted with, 'Shut up, Dee, and just do the scene.' You didn't argue with Charles when he had that tone of voice. I sat like an obedient dog waiting for its bone – or line – to be thrown to me. And I sucked.

I finished. Silence. 'What the hell was that?' Charles asked. I explained that I must've been thrown off by the last-second change of partners. He then launched into a half-hour diatribe expounding on the flexibility of his technique, and that this was exactly what he had taught us not to do, that I'd been out there working and picking up all these bad habits. I was losing the purity of the technique, and if I'm going to come to class, I am expected to work like everyone else and not be a prima donna ...

Here they came: the tears welled up and began to flow. And the next thing I knew, I had lost it. My God. I was yelling at Charles. I was yelling at my teacher, my guru. Actually, I was swearing at him like a truck driver. I was allowed my own diatribe: Don't talk to me like that, I didn't 'fake' this, I was doing my best, I hit my scenes most of the time, and if I can't make mistakes, what the hell is the class about then? I sucked because ...

Charles interrupted me and yelled, 'Because you judged!'

I stopped. 'What do you mean, I judged? I read the scene once, without inflection, no ideas.'

'Not your scene, Dee. Your partner. You judged your partner.' I was stunned, horrified, and disgusted with myself. That was absolutely what I had done. I had judged this newcomer as inadequate, and had paid for it with a bad performance. Gently, Charles pointed out his next cardinal rule: 'Don't judge,' and it applied to much more than the material. Whenever you judge anything connected to the creative process, and life is the greatest drama of all, the balance of energy gets thrown off and the flow stops. Don't judge the material, your partner, the location, the time, the weather, the wardrobe, whether you're required to arrive fifteen minutes early, or whatever life might throw at you – anything that will throw you out of alignment with your higher purpose and intention: to create truthfully from the core of your being. Judgment, Charles insisted, allowed you to bail out, not commit. It pulled you back from being at one with the experience, and placed you either in a superior or inferior attitude. Neither position served your main purpose, which was to be open to all the information needed to bring the character to life.

This made sense to me. It was just damn hard to catch yourself doing it. I tried to meditate on judgment – everyone was meditating back then. This was when it came into the mainstream, and all good little New Age actors were practicing it. But meditation was hell for me: you had to sit still. I was never good at sitting still. Take me to gymnastics or dance class or the playground, but don't ask me to sit still for five minutes. So I ventured into the other self-improvement craze of the 1970s LA scene: EST.

EST stood for Erhard Seminars Training. It was an intensive two-weekend process where yuppie leaders would walk you through endless exercises to uncover your bullshit, and to 'take responsibility for your life.' It was confrontational and dramatic and was natural for an actor, and I didn't have to sit still. One huge positive concept that I got from EST was that whatever happened just happened. It was a fact. Whatever emotional charge it still had for me, I was responsible for that association. I had judged the happening (usually as 'bad') and had become a victim of it. This really helped free me from being an emotional victim of my father's suicide.

The downside was that sessions were run like boot-camp training with guards at the doors who wouldn't let you out to take a pee. It was the belief of Werner Erhard that people escaped not facing their 'stuff' by leaving to 'piss it away.' Well, I have a bladder the size of a pea, and I often have to pee. This led to humiliating exchanges and failed opportunities for non-judgment with the 'assholes' at the door, trying to convince them that I wasn't 'running away from my shit' but simply 'running to the throne.'

The biggest gift from EST was seeing how much I was judging – and therefore, not loving – myself. I really had never realized how my poor family with its emotional abuse issues, alcohol problems and Midwestern ethics had created the continual self-judgment of 'not being as good, smart, or acceptable' as everyone else professionally. It crossed into my personal life as well. Several successful men would ask me out. We would go to great restaurants, and they would spend a huge amount of money to court me. Since I was never comfortable with myself, I felt that I didn't deserve this kind of attention. It always felt like I was in some kind of surreal movie and that this wasn't really happening to me. I couldn't figure out why I had this 'less than' feeling when I was creating so much in my career. Years later I would look at my old pictures and tapes with my daughter, and realize that I never saw myself as pretty. It made me sad to think that I didn't appreciate my true worth, but lived in the limited reality of my false perception. That's why I longed to be acting in every moment: I didn't judge myself while I was a character in a film. But as soon as I returned to real life, that feeling would creep back. I struggled back then to unite the non-judgment of craft and self.

This was, however, an interesting dichotomy of Sir Charles. He understood non-judgment thoroughly when it came to the creative side, but didn't understand or practice it at all as it applied to the movie business. Everyone who needed to hire us as actors was simply an imbecile. Hardly a class went by that he didn't regale us with four-letter descriptions of how stupid, inept, clueless, and idiotic most casting directors, directors, agents, and producers really were. It was sheer luck that anything got made at all, and they wouldn't know talent from their own asshole. Obviously Charles had been burned in the past by a lot of these 'somebodies.' And obviously this judgment about the business of making movies had stopped the flow of his acting career. This fact didn't escape me even while I was attending class and getting so much out of his creative approach to acting. It was common sense that you couldn't hate the business if you wanted to succeed in it. And you couldn't be angry and create the life you wanted.

As much as I loved Charles, he could get pissy and downright hurtful. I think the frustration of having all that talent and not having it acknowledged was often too much for him to handle. There were times when he would just simply lose it. I distinctly remember a class where he launched into a tirade about an actor's scene.

'What are you DOING?' Charles roared. He shot to his feet. This was not a good sign. He never stood up. As he began to pace like a caged animal, the diatribe escalated from 'You don't have a clue what you're doing' to 'How the hell can you sit there like an idiot and act from these ideas?' to him turning to all of us and calling us 'stupid, anal little creatures that will never be actors.'

'Get out! All of you get the hell out of my classroom.' Everyone got up silently and made their way to the door. As I was about to leave, he yelled once more, 'You're stupid!'

In that moment I lost it. I turned, the tears started, and I yelled, 'You're an asshole sometimes! We're not stupid. We're scared. And we're trying. And we depend on you to guide us. Belittling us doesn't help anyone. And don't you ever call me stupid again!' There was dead silence as those still remaining watched to see the final showdown between Dee and Charles. As in all good acting, you couldn't have predicted his comeback in a million years. Charles started laughing. At first I thought he was laughing at me. But he was simply ... laughing. 'What are you laughing about?' I said in relief.

'I'm laughing because ... we're ALL assholes, and brilliant, and passionate, and I really love you guys.'

Then we both started crying. Charles was, to say the least, an enigma. But try as he might, up to the last days of his teaching career, he still thought 'they' were against us. He should have called my grandma. As Gram Bow used to say, 'Love life and it loves you back.'

Because I was aware of this fact and still had that Midwest

Pollyanna affection for most people I met, I continued making contacts and moving ahead with my career. From the acting end, Charles had given me a way to consistently create what I had always done naturally: be in the moment and act instinctively. His formula would keep me in balance: I could depend on my technique, my beingness, and me consistently. That kept me focused on my end of the equation and out of judgment about the other end, whether it was the material, actors, or industry types. I could remain in the flow.

About this time, I landed an incredible guest-star part in the series *Lou Grant*. The character was a hooker who was trying to get out of the 'life' by passing a real-estate exam for her license. She got right up to the point of making this transition, but just couldn't quite pull it off. The last scene of the show was the woman defeated by circumstances and going back to turn yet another trick, always thinking she would eventually get there, maybe next year. The newspaper was doing a story on her journey of coming to Los Angeles, failing as an actress, and getting 'hooked' into the easy money of prostitution. This was an incredible part and opportunity.

When I walked into the first audition, there were many recognizable television actresses sitting in the waiting room. I could feel that familiar judgment of not belonging and not being good enough shift my energy. I could almost feel myself giving up. But I desperately wanted this part, and not because it would be an important gig, but this character had taken me over and I wanted to be her. In fact I was already her! I went out to the hall and sat by myself. If I stayed in the energy of those actresses, whom I greatly admired, I would never keep my focus and stay in my power. I made myself take deep breaths. The best performance I turned in that day was just keeping Dee grounded. And I gave a great reading, even though I wondered if that would be the sole criteria with this mix of ladies. The callback was even tougher – three even bigger actresses were auditioning with those of us called back from the previous day. You knew how far you were up the importance ladder if you didn't have to come in for the first round.

I did what I do well enough that I had a third, fourth, and fifth callback. They must have been sitting in those casting meetings going, 'Who the hell is Dee Wallace?'

'I don't know her.'

'Everyone else is so much better known.'

'Yeah, but she's the best one for the part.'

'Okay. Hire the kid.'

I mean, really, they had pretty much seen the same performance five times in a row. It wasn't how big or recognizable or even how good you were; it was how right you were for the part back then. You were judged by your talent, not your track record. Newcomers had much more of a chance to 'break in.'

I booked the role. It was an amazing experience: the script, the other actors, and the director. Everybody was brilliant. However, there was one little glitch during a scene where I had to use several props. The script girl approached to remind me of all the little nuances of the scene.

'Okay,' she began in a very abrupt, businesslike manner, 'on the word "the" you picked up the pencil. On the word "and" you erased something about halfway down the page. Be sure when you get up that you turn to the left instead of the right, and then turn back over your left shoulder. We may need to intercut there. On the word "test" you put the pencil in your mouth ...'

I went into total sheer panic, and got pissed off at having to think of any of these minutiae. Those instructions put me directly in my head and out of the flow, out of my beingness. I immediately started judging the stupidity of imposing such a complicated scheme on such an emotional scene.

Seven takes later the director approached me. Instant self-judgment arose and again, flashes from *The Streets of San Francisco* came back. But he was very kind, very understanding.

'What's going on, sweetie? You've nailed everything else on the first take.' I explained how I was worried about carrying out the script girl's instructions and was so focused on the props and hitting my mark that I kept messing up. I saw him do a very internal, but immediate, burn. He looked at me. 'Screw it. Don't worry about the damn props. Just act.'

Freedom! Joy! Bliss! I had received a pardon from the mental prison and could move back into the field of flow. There was one more take and we were done. And the amazing thing was that I did it perfectly – every prop, on every line, and in perfect synchronicity. I had learned yet again that when I was balanced, it all happened. When I was in my head, it was hard work. I shared this in class. 'Yes,' Charles confirmed, 'you just have to say "Fuck it," and then it happens.'

Lou Grant also gave me a great opportunity to put a string of scenes together in a very focused amount of time. It was the process of how to gauge the energy from one scene in class to ten scenes in twelve hours. Not only did you have to be aware of balancing your emotional portrayal, but the sheer physical energetic challenge was sometimes daunting. On the larger scale, I was also learning to balance self with success, and self with family. I was beginning to understand that I couldn't live, eat, and breathe acting 24/7 without burning out. All work and no play made Deanna unbalanced.

Six weeks later, my friends and I gathered around the television to watch the *Lou Grant* episode. This was a lovely little ritual that happened every time any of us appeared. We were supported whether we crashed or not. Every actor needs that. It's a kind of friendship safety net. The episode ended. I didn't have to ask. I knew. I knew as clearly as the little girl knew riding in the back seat of the car after my dance recital so many years ago. I was good. I was really, really good. My friends applauded. I think we even cracked open a bottle of champagne. My family called, as they always did, to celebrate the victory. Gram Bow, back to her old feisty self, Mom, my younger brother, and my aunt had all assembled to watch and cheer me and call to yell whoopee. I always waited for those calls. My family's love and support meant the world to me and kept me grounded. Even they knew this performance was a little more special than the others I'd given. And I knew that I had turned another corner in my acting career.

The next morning confirmed that intuition. The flow kept coming with a call from my agency. 'Dee,' my agent's excited voice greeted me, 'Lynn Stalmaster's people saw *Lou Grant* last night and want to bring you in to read for Blake Edwards. It's for a part opposite Dudley Moore in his new movie *10*! This is big, Dee. This is what we've been waiting for. They're seeing the last round of girls today. Just drop everything and go.'

I was stunned. Blake Edwards was a really big movie director. My agent messengered the sides over to me. I memorized them (without any inflection, of course), threw myself together, and drove to the studio. I was nervous and excited (the same energy, except nervousness has more fear attached). Just do what you know, Dee, I kept saying to myself. Do the technique.

I walked in, met Mr Edwards, and stated rather bluntly that I would like to do the audition and then talk. Fine. No problem. I hadn't had the material very long, and I had judged that fact. It gave me a convenient excuse to drop the ball in case I didn't 'show up.' I was flying through the scene, and I was so high that I got lost in the zone and couldn't remember the next line. 'Line, please,' I said.

Blake stopped the scene. 'It's great; let's take it from the top.'

I went into more judgment. Why couldn't someone just have given me the line? I began again. I swear to God, at the exact same place I forgot the line again. Before anyone could say anything, I threw my hand out like a traffic cop and said, 'Just give me the line.' They did. The rest of the scene was perfect. We talked for five minutes, and I was out the door. When I got home, there was a message from my agent. I had booked the job. Good for you, Deanna, I thought. And you did it your way, as old Blue Eyes would say.

I was on my way to Las Hadas, Mexico, to be featured in a film with Dudley Moore, which was being directed by Blake Edwards. Two superstars. And I had barely entered my third year in the business. As I was preparing for this trip, I realized that one scene called for me to be in bed, after failed sex, with Dudley Moore. I called my agent. They assured me that if I was expected to do nudity, it would have to be in the contract. Whew. The Midwest family definitely wasn't ready for that kind of exposure. Since no one from the studio had contacted me, I figured that I was to buy my own underwear for the scene. Most independent films required you to bring wardrobe from your own closet. What did I know? I actually think the wardrobe people found it rather endearing that I showed up with my own lingerie, albeit a little naive. Needless to say, this was a multimillion-dollar production: they had clothes for me.

On the other hand, that unknowingness, which was my own special kind of knowingness, helped me create flow in other areas of the production. It was the first day of shooting on the most beautiful beach in Las Hadas, Mexico. I thought I had died and gone to heaven just being there. We were all put up in marvelous villas, and a car had picked me up and dropped me at the beach location where we would be shooting the scene where Mary Lewis walks across very hot sand and brings the camera to George Webber, Dudley's character. When I arrived, there were several large trailers: one of them had Dudley's name, and the other had 'Ms Derek' emblazoned on the card in the window. Little did I know that my agent hadn't negotiated a dressing room for me. On my first day at this glorious location, Mr Edwards came over to say hello. He asked if everything was all right.

'Yes,' I gushed, 'and thank you very much. Just one thing,

where's my trailer?'

Of course I hadn't been assigned one, but I didn't know that. So my intention of being my happy creative self manifested a trailer right there on the spot. Blake looked at his assistant, Tony Adams, and asked where my trailer was. Tony didn't skip a beat. 'Ah, it hasn't arrived yet, Mr Edwards,' he lied. 'I'll get right on it.' Bo graciously shared her trailer with me until mine got there. Yep. What I didn't know helped me. I asked and I received. Sweet.

Shooting *10* was one of the highlights of my career. I found myself working with genuinely kind, loving, and talented people like Julie Andrews, Brian Dennehy, and of course, the amazing Dudley Moore. I was in heaven. Not only was the part a little gem, but I was working opposite an actor who loved to be in the moment. Dudley came out of improvisation and would clown around and veer off the script into the weirdest places. For example, in the scene where we enter his room, the script flatly stated that he was *leading me in and down the hall to the sleeping quarters*. While we were waiting for the director's cue, Dudley was tickling me and we were clowning around and I was telling him to stop, that I had to be in my actor's focus. Well, he suddenly pulled me to him and planted this friendly kiss on me and we then heard 'Action.' So mid-kiss he kicks the door open, and we stumble down the hallway entwined in arms and lips, stumble and slowly fall over the balcony onto the bed. Backwards. Again, thank God for my dance background. Well, that got us laughing so much that taking our clothes off became endearing in our acted-out alcoholic states, and this led into a huge emotional arc that dovetailed from hilarity to tenderness and then embarrassment. It was like an exercise from acting class. Totally unexpected and just perfect. I often joked that I just became Mary Lewis and held on for the joy ride. And it was always just that. You never knew where Dudley would take you, but you knew it would be fun and you were safely strapped in. I vigilantly monitored my judgment, kept myself in balance, and had fun!

Dudley and I would have discussions about techniques and planning out the beats. 'Not for us,' he quipped. 'They know the moments they're moving into. We discover the moments when we're in them.' Dudley and I were in the 'improv' of life itself. I loved this man! Charles called it the Hummingbird Quality: you never knew where the character was buzzing off to or flitting around. You just watched the dance of knowingness: the moments of life being born.

I tried to stay in that dance even when I was scared to death. As we were starting the big bedroom scene, Blake came over and sat down by me. I had a robe on over a halter-top and panties. He looked at me for what seemed to be hours. 'So, how do you feel about playing this nude?' he asked rather innocently. I felt my little Kansas heart drop right to my knees, but somehow gallantly held on to my composure. Keep the balance, girl, I told myself. Don't look like the scared asshole you feel like right now. Visions of my grandmother watching the film and hanging herself flew through my head.

'Well, Mr Edwards,' I started tentatively, 'I think it's wrong for the character. I mean, he hasn't been able to get it up and I wouldn't want to flaunt it in his face. Everyone else is nude in the movie. And, bottom line, I make my money doing commercials, so if you can guarantee me three more pictures so I can make a living, I'll try.' I blinked my eyes winningly.

There was a really long pause. 'Okay,' he smiled, and walked away. I was so discombobulated; I was Mary Lewis at that point. Dudley came over, put his arm around me, and said, 'You're safe with me. You know that.' How did he know the magic words?

Eventually, everything came off under my robe because the camera kept catching my underwear. I gave up my resistance, trusted, and committed. I followed Dudley through a maze of scripted and improvised lines. We ended the take and everyone waited in silence for the God Blake Edwards to hand down his decree: 'Well, I don't know who the fuck wrote this scene, but we're gonna print it!' I had taken my first step into the big time, energetically and physically. I trusted now that I could hold my own, stay balanced, and rely on my formula to always see me through.

After my final scene, Blake took me aside before I left town. We went off to a quiet secluded section of the soundstage while everyone was preparing the next scene. I had grown to love this gentle giant of a creative force. And I felt safe with him. I was anxious to hear what he would need from me.

'You're a really good actress, Dee. I want to send you to see my agent.'

'Oh my God, Mr Edwards. Thanks. I don't know what to say,' I said and gave him a big hug.

I was honored, and I dutifully went to see Marty Baum at CAA, one of the biggest and most lucrative agencies in town at that time. CAA looked at every frame of film I had, said they thought I was terrific, and to come back when I was making $500,000 a year. This is it, I thought. I will never be accepted as the star I want to be now. It hadn't occurred to me that my self-judgment was quietly sabotaging me in that moment. It was like the scene in class, except the other actor was … me. I never felt a part of 'that group,' whether it was the popular kids in high school or the successful movie stars of Hollywood. And if I didn't know I was, the Universe simply couldn't create that outcome for me.

Back in Los Angeles after the film wrapped, Blake invited me to join Julie, Dudley, and himself for dinner. I used some excuse about already having fixed plans. It was just too hard to join that élite group. As the song goes, 'I'd gone about as far as I could go.' I guess I had to be sure that the light wasn't too bright. And I didn't realize I was creating more of the reality of that belief every moment. The turndown by CAA was a huge energetic blow. You mean … I'm not good enough? You're judging me as not big enough? I got defensive and angry and hurt. If Blake Edwards couldn't turn this corner for me, who could? I won't need you then, I thought. Can you hear the judgment? I couldn't then. But I began to slightly dislike the movie business that Charles so despised.

There weren't a lot of acting gigs showing up. Forging a movie career took time. But a former TV director of mine called and asked, as a favor to him, if I would do an episode of *Chips*.

Hmm, I thought, from a Blake Edwards movie to *Chips*. Well, what the hell, a girl's got to work and I hated just standing around waiting. So I said yes.

My head agent called to see if I'd gone loco. 'Dee, seriously,' he began. 'There's a protocol in this town. You can't do a major film with a major director and do *Chips* next. You just can't.' The Barbra Streisand lyric, 'Everybody says don't, everybody says don't … well I say do,' began blasting in my head. It had been two months since I had worked.

'You have anything on the horizon?' I asked. Silence. 'I'll take that as a no.'

He sighed. 'Make the best deal you can.' He hung up on me and didn't talk to me for weeks. But that little angel of mine knew exactly what she was doing. I was to co-star with a man named Christopher Stone. He was a really big, established actor who also came in to do the director a favor, and proceeded to direct me the entire week. I thought he was a little pompous; he thought I was a little green.

As fate would have it, we had to ride back to the trailer together after the last day of location filming, and he began questioning me about my credits. I mentioned that I had done this great episode of *Lou Grant* that led to … I never got the sentence finished. He turned and looked at me as if I had just changed from the ugly stepsister to Cinderella.

'Oh my God, you played that hooker. That was you.' I

confirmed the obvious. 'Jesus!' he exclaimed. 'You were brilliant. I even called my wife in to watch you. I told her you were going to be a really big star. This is so synchronistic. This is amazing. You were amazing.' I thanked him, got out of the van, got changed, and drove home. When I got there, two dozen red roses were already waiting on my front step.

Chapter Five

The Instinctive Response

Dee Wallace was doing just great in Hollywood. Deanna Bowers was missing her family who were halfway across the country. Family had always been and would always be the most important aspect of my life. The local Hallmark Cards shop was consistently depleted from the amount of correspondence I mailed back each week. I missed Gram Bow. I missed Mom. I missed the fall leaves and the humidity and yes, even the winter snow. I just missed that yellow brick road that was home.

And then the roses came, followed by a phone call two hours later. It was Christopher Stone, calling to ask me out.

'You're married,' I said.

'Getting divorced,' he replied.

'How the hell did you get my phone number?' I asked. The second assistant director had handed it over – something they weren't supposed to do.

'And how did you get my address?' I demanded. My answering service had given it to him! What? That was a real no-no. That was a breach of contract, a security risk.

'Yeah,' admitted Chris. 'But I knew the guy.'

Right. He didn't know the guy at all. But I was to learn during what became an eighteen-year love affair that Chris could get blood out of a turnip, the best table at Caesars in Las Vegas, and the phone number for the girl who had starred in *Lou Grant*.

'I want to take you to dinner.' I figured that couldn't hurt. 'Tomorrow night?'

'I already have plans tomorrow night.'

There wasn't a moment's pause. 'Okay. We'll go the night after.' I had plans already, but was free on Saturday. 'Saturday is my card night. I've been playing cards with the same guys on Saturday nights for ten years.'

'Call me next week and we'll try to find a night,' I said.

Again, there was no pause suggesting any kind of thought process, just pure instinct. 'Never mind,' he answered. 'I'll pick you up at seven on Saturday.' He definitely knew how to play cards, and had played that hand really well.

Saturday came and he took me to Le Petit Chateau, a very fine restaurant which was to become 'our place.' He was greeted like a king, given a private table, ordered a fabulous bottle of wine, and began flashing that already famous smile that made millions of women dizzy. I decided I wasn't going to be that easy. I still remembered 'the asshole who tried to direct me all week.' But he proved to be charming, absolutely charming. Chris was kind, intelligent, spiritual, and manly. He knew how to make a woman feel like a princess, and I was more than willing to be his Queen for a Day.

He wined and dined me, and won me over enough to open up the possibility that I might let him get closer. As he said, he was ending a divorce, living alone in a studio transition apartment, but he had an amazing aura that suggested he could handle anything. You instantly felt safe with Chris.

He took me home, walked me to the door, thanked me for the fabulous night, and walked away. I mused at the fact that he knew how to play the opening love scene: cut to man and woman at dinner, cut to drinking, cut to laughter, cut to slight touching, cut to car pulling up, cut to man saying goodnight, cut to girl wanting more. And I did.

We had made plans for the following night: dinner and a movie. It was a love story, of course, and when we walked to the door, he leaned in and gave me a very light, soft, full kiss. My knees went weak, the music swelled and the rest, as they say, is history. I had found my family, my port in the storm, my soul mate and my safety net.

Within three weeks we were living together, and he was starting his tactical maneuvers to get a diamond ring on my very bare left hand. I wasn't ready. I wasn't sure. It was too fast. My head was ruling my heart with all the excuses my mother would've brought up.

'I'll wait.' He flashed that smile.

Two months into the relationship, he wanted to look for rings again.

'I'm not ready.'

'I'll wait.'

Four months and the same exchange took place. Six months, ditto. Finally, at nine months I was so bloody in love with the guy that I caved. And then something happened that was right out of a fairytale.

We went back to a store where we had gone antiquing about four months earlier. We both loved antiques and while we had been there, Chris had spied one particular ring. We both loved it: it was a 1920s platinum antique setting with diamonds. I must have had a fabulous life in the twenties, because I'm drawn to everything in that era. But I simply wasn't ready for a ring at the time. The owner remembered us (we were awfully cute together), and asked what we were looking for. We explained about the ring and that we were disappointed but not surprised that it was no longer in the case. His face went slightly white. He turned around, retrieved a box, and opened it. There was the ring: our ring. A woman had put it on layaway for ... yep, four months, and had just called to say she wouldn't be taking it. She had called half an hour before we walked into the store. Needless to say, we bought it. It seemed like magic.

And it was. Chris just lived his life from a place of synchronicity. He put out an intention, and what he wanted showed up. I think it had largely to do with him just knowing who he was. What was naiveté for me was conscious living for him. He was involved in a philosophy called Conceptology. In retrospect, it was *The Secret*,

Positive Thinking, and Creating Your Life all rolled into one. It was my first introduction to the philosophy of positive living. It was great to have this common ground of discussion and guidance to share. From the beginning, Chris would be my balance and guidance through some tumultuous waters that lay ahead.

I was the quintessential cliché for an actress: there were very few gray areas. Life for Dee was pretty black or white. I was either phenomenally happy or hysterically in histrionics. Chris, on the other hand, was pretty unaffected by most situations. Maybe it was his marine training. After all, he certainly seized the moment with me. He was just always more in the emotional middle. And that brought balance into our home and into my life. As I've said, there wasn't anything, anyplace, or anyone that I didn't feel safe around when I was with him. We would share eighteen glorious years together, create a beautiful daughter, and work in numerous productions as co-stars.

The beginning of our professional life together (after *Chips*) was a little film called *The Howling*. Doing this film was a huge decision for me. During my climb up the ladder, I had moved to bigger agencies that were much more specific about the projects their actors did. There was much discussion about whether this was the kind of project I should be doing at this time in my career and with this director ... blah, blah. The decisions that had been instinctual before were now more involved. Before, the question whether I wanted to work was a no-brainer. Now, just working wasn't the issue. I had to build a career, the right way. All this questioning made me doubt everything: Did I pick the right agents, the right movies, the right hairstyle, etc.? I forgot it was really about me and about my knowing.

This was clearly demonstrated to us in one of Charles' acting exercises. We were all given the same scene and asked to prepare it over the course of the week. Everyone was instructed to break down the beats, work the moments – in other words, prepare it from the mental point of view. The next week we watched that scene acted out twelve times and essentially the same way. Everyone had basically taken the identical approach – the good but safe mental rendition of the material.

The following week we were all given another scene in class, told to read it with our partner, and then put it down. That day we watched twelve totally different renditions of it. Half of them were breathlessly exciting, half merely adequate. But they were all original, based on an actor's instinctual response from his or her unique knowingness. That's our blank page; the mind gives us computer readouts of collective averages. If asked to do the scene again, we would've come up with slightly different renditions, because each moment is different and so are we.

And this applies to real-life decisions as well. So I took my problem with some trepidation to class to air it out. It was probably not the best place to ask about the business end of the business, but I needed to apply some acting 'wisdom' to the situation. Charles again went into a half-hour riff about the jerks in the business. I heard every major negative belief about all the people needed to help build my career: they aren't creative, they won't look out for you because they only want to make a buck, they think they're God but it's their ego, they want to use you … I waited until the master had run out of steam.

'Aren't those kinds of negative, limiting beliefs?' I asked hesitantly. 'I mean, I don't think all of them are instinctively that way, Charles.'

He paused. 'That's the point, Dee. They're not coming from their instinct. Instinct is a true, emotional gut reaction from your deep knowing. Those assholes are mentally jerking off with their ego and at your expense.'

I took a deep breath. My integrity had to speak up. 'I don't entirely believe that, Charles. I know, as you have taught us, that nothing is black and white for actors. Everyone is creating from their own fears and perspectives. So that has to apply to all the people in the industry, too.'

I could 'hear' the air in class. I think twenty-two people stopped breathing all at once. The air was thick with 'What's gonna happen next?' And the next moment took our breath away. Charles shared a part of his soul we had never seen: the vulnerable part.

'I guess I'm reacting out of ego right now, aren't I?' the master said quietly. He paused for a moment. 'Maybe I'm doing exactly what I am accusing them of – making a judgment from fear.'

It was quiet for what seemed like hours. And then, as if picking up a scene in the middle of the take, he moved right back into his passionate probing regarding whether to take the film. 'What do YOU want, Dee? What do your instincts tell you? What does your heart want to do? Didn't I teach you to stay out of your fucking head?' he bellowed.

Damn. He was right. But like his forgetting, it was getting harder to be instinctive when all these 'gods' were telling me to be afraid of the choices I made. I wanted to do the film. I just didn't know if what I wanted was 'right.' I could trust my instincts in my acting roles, but as I've said, my real-life role was more of a challenge. I often couldn't distinguish my still, small voice from their loud, booming caution. Somehow instinct must be the core of my guidance system, but it was becoming subconsciously harder to listen while trying to avoid the genetic predisposition from my father: to get right to the point of winning, and fail. So far, I had held those sneaky little self-defeating cells at bay, but I could feel them multiplying now like a cancer growth.

But I trusted my mentor. I had a formula: Know, trust, intuit, flow, channel. That works for you, Dee, I kept reminding myself – try to apply it in acting AND life. So I bit the bullet and made the decision. I would do *The Howling*. It was my first real leading role and it was a great emotional ride. I loved our producer, Dan Blatt. I loved the director, Joe Dante. They agreed not to add any additional nudity to the final script. They agreed that my character would never have to appear as a werewolf. And it was the most money I had ever made. It felt good. The balance was back. Charles had helped me go with my natural instinct, from which everything flowed. I had shifted into the masculine, analytical left brain, the ego, the planning zone; and Charles had brought me back to the right side of my brain, the feminine side – my instinct.

I was preparing dinner when the call came. It was Dan Blatt, and he had some questions about scheduling, etc. I asked him how it was going, and he admitted that he was thrilled with how everything was coming together.

'There's just one problem: we can't find an actor to play your husband.'

'Well, what are you looking for?' I asked.

'He needs to be macho and really good-looking, but with a sensitive side. And he needs to be really well built.'

I'm sure you're ahead of me already. How had this not occurred to me? In twenty seconds, I devised a plan. 'Hmm. You know, I worked with this actor on a TV show ... what's his name? I think it was Chris something ... Stone or Smith or some such name. It sounds like he might be right if you can find him.' Dan got off the phone with a very clear intention. And he found him.

They tracked Chris down; he went in, auditioned, and got the part. The next day the phone rang. It was Dan.

'Hi, Dan,' I chirped happily.

'Dee? I'm sorry. I must've dialed the wrong number. I was calling that guy you recommended – Chris Stone. He was great. We hired him.'

'I know, Dan, and you didn't call the wrong number.' Again, there was that long silence that everyone in Hollywood knows only too well when the jig is up.

'Oh, shit!' I heard him exclaim. 'You guys are going to gang up on me.'

'Look at it this way, Dan. You only have to get one trailer.'

How lucky could a girl get? I was engaged to my leading

man; we were on location in beautiful northern California, with a great director and producer. I mean really, how good does it get? I just had to figure out how to balance Dee and Deanna: I'm playing a character that almost gets free and then has to sacrifice herself at the end, while I'm also drinking alone because Chris is doing a nude scene with another actress, and I'm exhausted from the day's shoot yet still going out to eat with a lover who wants to play because he has a lot of time off. Piece of cake. Know, trust, intuit, flow, channel. Right.

And so we immersed ourselves in the shooting of *The Howling*, a story of a man who is trying to tame the natural instincts of the werewolf into a socially acceptable formula package: the left/right brain, male/female, logic/instinct dilemma that's been around since the beginning. If the doctor could just merge the two sides to help them channel their urges, think of the possibilities in using this for the treatment of regular, screwed-up people. Indeed. Always the English teacher, I saw the metaphorical meaning in the most bizarre of stories, and now how everything was a metaphor for consciousness.

The Howling wasn't a mere werewolf saga; it was a parable about natural instincts threatening individual and societal norms, and the battle of the psyche in determining at any given moment which side would prevail. It was Jekyll and Hyde in fur and snouts. I was fighting in the movie the very fears that I had kept at bay in my life. Even the ending represents this focus of mine. Remember, my character wasn't supposed to appear as a werewolf. But at the pre-screenings, everyone had written on their cards that they'd like to see the star get furry. I was off shooting *Cujo*. Joe said they didn't need me, just my consent. 'Fine,' I said. 'Just try to make her a little different. Try to give her a little vulnerability because she's fought so hard against them.' And that is how the Bambi werewolf at the end was born.

The Howling was also about those nebulous lines of instinct and sexual energy. They often got confusing for me. I was very concerned that line didn't get blurred between Chris and his she-wolf.

'Pupper,' my blond god said gently, 'to borrow a line from Paul Newman, "why would I go out for hamburger when I have steak at home?"' The boy knew how to work it. As he came tripping in at 4:00 A.M. to a rather drunk fiancée, I asked him how the shoot went. 'We froze our butts off; she has droopy boobs and bad breath. I love you. Go to sleep.' I did.

For the first time in my life I was participating in a healthy, sexual, spiritual relationship between two successful people who were individually fulfilled. It was a revelation to me. I had seen parts of this mix in my family, but never the complete picture. With this realization my doubts about being deserving raised their annoying little heads. I pushed them away and buried them … for now. I can make this work. I do deserve it all.

So we spent six weeks working together, or should I say shooting together. Chris would work on his part, fill in his blanks, practice the lines, and get prepared. I, on the other hand, would learn my lines and agree to run them with him. We worked well together: he was mental in his work and instinctual in his life. I was instinctual in my work and becoming more and more mental in life. I was a nut job. He was in balance. Perfect marriage. And often Joe Dante sought Chris's help to maintain that balance. One of my co-stars in *The Howling* also worked with an opposing technique. Most of the time, we could move fluidly through the discovery of the material; one day it just didn't happen. This other actor had some very specific ideas of how he wanted the scene to play. It's not that I was opposed to his ideas on principle; they just didn't work for my character.

Discussions and more discussions took place. Joe was helping (as delicately as he could) to guide us through what was a potential minefield of stalemates. 'Let's just try it,' he finally suggested. I felt intimidated by the whole scenario, but I forced myself to commit. We finished the rehearsal. My co-star was ecstatic. I looked at Joe.

'Well,' he smiled, 'it works, but it's not great.'

That was all I needed to be thrown into my own den of wolves: my fears and self-judgments. I began to feel that panic. Why didn't I know what to do with this scene? Why wasn't the technique working? What the hell do you do when you're emotionally naked in front of a crew that wants to go home early for a change? My emotions began to escalate.

'Let's just shoot it,' the other actor suggested.

I lost it. 'Shoot what?' I demanded. 'A not-great scene?' I looked at Joe. 'I need a few minutes.'

I went to my trailer. My co-star went to his. And Joe called Chris. He arrived on the set some minutes later and entered our trailer to find a very distraught fiancée.

'Pupper,' he said, taking me into his arms, 'repeat after me: "It's only a movie, it's only a movie …"'

I broke a little bit of a smile. 'Yes,' I said meekly, 'but it's my movie.' He asked me, if there was one thing that would help me, what would it be? 'Charles,' I answered without hesitation. 'I need to talk to Charles.'

And so I did. I called him at the acting studio. He was getting ready to go into class but he took my call. I explained my dilemma, my panic, my end-of-the-rope, I-don't-know-what-I'm-doing-wrong stream of consciousness.

'Dee! Shut up,' he ordered me. I did. He began walking me through the technique. 'Is your energy high?'

'Yes!'

'Are you throwing it?'

'Yes!'

'Are you connecting?'

'Yes!'

'Then what idea did you come in with?'

I froze. My God, he was right! I had come in with an idea and I hadn't even realized it. I was so busy trying to be sure the other actor's ideas didn't affect me that I had sabotaged myself uncon-sciously by choosing one of my own.

'Oh my God, Charles,' I stammered. 'Why did I do that?'

'It happens, Dee. Forget it and go be brilliant.'

I wasn't. I couldn't get all the way back to that blank page of nothingness where no preconceived ideas exist: that place of all possibilities. I didn't really know at that point if this was about me in the new moment, or was I trying to keep the old idea out? I never moved back into that space of total trust where my talent could create truthfulness out of nothing again; my instinctive response had been clouded by my fears. In the final edit, the scene never made it into the picture.

When I got home that night, I thanked Chris for being there for me. I shared with him how embarrassed I was about my emotions and how I just couldn't shoot a scene that wasn't truthful.

'It's okay, Pupper. You do whatever you have to do to stay in your integrity. That's what makes you great.'

And that's one really important principle we shared: integrity. For both of us, this was of utmost importance. If I felt like I was leaving my integrity, I felt lost: I would have abandoned myself. I kept my word and expected everyone else to keep theirs. That's the way you did it back in Kansas. That was the most important aspect in a person's character besides being loving.

Sometimes that integrity, coupled with my naiveté, caused problems. For example, there was a wonderful barn scene where my character finally realizes the mess she's in, that everyone is probably going to eat her, but that the doctor meant well. It was 4:00 A.M.; we were at a ranch on the far outskirts of LA, and it was freezing. I walked into the barn already in emotional Lalaland, and looked up to see several women with rather large bare breasts hanging over the railing. The right brain and the left brain were fighting to understand what the hell was going on here.

'The studio wants more nudity for Europe,' Joe explained.

'No. My contract reads: "no more nudity than the present script." I won't do it.' A few more minutes of discussion ensued. I was torn between being judged as a difficult actress or judged later for being in a B movie with titties flying everywhere. Dan was called to the set.

At 4:00 A.M., Mr Blatt came flying through the ranch gate, pulled up to the barn, got out and slammed his car door. Dust was flying everywhere, literally and figuratively. He stomped into the barn, took one look around, and said, 'She's right, it's stupid.' He turned around, got into his car, and drove away. I will never forget him for that.

Dan Blatt was a man of integrity and a man of his word. He always had your back, or he explained why he couldn't. And in that moment, he confirmed to me beyond a shadow of a doubt that I could live in my integrity and be safe, heard, and honored. I could be Deanna Bowers and win. It was an enormous gift, and it helped bury those quiet little fears of insecurity that I had pushed down – and kept them buried for a precious long time.

I think what I appreciated most about Dan was his respect for others. He didn't listen to my needs, concerns, and thoughts because I was the star of his film. He respected people and the process of creation that was individual to everyone. I witnessed him showing the same respect for members of the crew and his own family. He would listen, assess, and take action in the appropriate manner. Sometimes that meant the decision went your way, and sometimes it didn't. But you knew you were respected, heard, and honored. And so, of course, you desperately wanted to give your best for Dan. He always supported me following my truth.

Not everyone shared Dan's understanding of truth and integrity. When I got back from shooting *The Howling*, I was sent to audition for a movie of the week. The scenes concerned a woman who first finds her husband after committing suicide, and then hours later when she is talking with the police. I went in and played those scenes in total truthfulness. I know. I lived them. When I was a junior in high school, I found my father in my bed, blood flowing from slit wrists after his first suicide attempt. I handled it, but two hours later I was at a neighbor's house hysterical.

I finished the audition and looked up. No one said anything. Finally the director asked, 'Why did you play the scenes that way? Why did you play the first scene when you find him so in control, and the last scene with the police so emotionally distraught?'

'Because that's the truth. That's the way it happens. You handle it, and then you lose it.' I proceeded to share with them my personal experience.

He looked at me and replied, 'I see. Well, play it the way people THINK it would happen.'

'I'm sorry,' I said, 'I just can't do that. If I can't play it truthfully, you'll have to give the part to someone else.' And they did. And I really didn't care.

I celebrated returning to class, to my safe haven where I knew I would hear, and share, the truth. By this time, my experience on movie sets had become a valuable tool for Charles' teaching; and always, I learned as much as everyone did from his insight and ability to explain life through spirituality and energy. He believed that we attracted parts and projects that were an extension of ourselves and what we needed to emotionally work out: a mirror, if you will. The werewolves were my demons, my fears that I was trying to conquer. It made sense to me. We really are all living in our own horror film depending on what we're running from. I realized that I hadn't won the fight for right-eousness at the end of this film. 'Don't worry, Dee,' Charles smiled. 'It's only a movie.' But it was the movie that at this point characterized my career, and it was about being safe. Success was attracting a lot more hungry animals and more fears and doubts than I expected.

I spent four weeks getting back into physical and artistic shape after six weeks of pigging out and compromising on a working set. It is the nature of the beast that you sometimes eat donuts or junk food and at other times compromise your technique, merely due to time constraints, locations, unending hours, and the director's vision. Charles kept hammering his lessons into us: the purity of intention, no ideas or expectations, energy, balance, and trusting the instinct, until I was back on the bike again.

A few months later, the film studio held a big premier in New York City. Both families decided to meet there and have one big family gathering. Even my beloved Gram Bow, always ready for a good time, showed up. We all went into the theater and took our seats. I had educated my family on the nudity, so they wouldn't be taken aback. Thank God Gram Nichols couldn't make it. The theater lights dimmed; the picture began. I was a nervous wreck, watching and trying to feel the vibes of their reactions. The big love scene came on, and I held my breath. No one turned around. No one moved.

Then, out of the darkness I heard my grandmother's voice: 'Why Christopher Stone, shame on you!' The audience roared. We laughed about it for years. The picture was well received by family, friends, and critics.

I remember opening the *Hollywood Reporter* the next day to read the review. They liked it. And they loved me. 'Chris!' I yelled, 'They gave me great reviews.'

He smiled that Clark Gable smile, kissed me, and delivered one of the most important lines in my life. 'Just remember, Pupper. If you believe the good ones, you have to believe the bad ones, too.' In other words, you are the only one who really knows. You are the only one who can really judge the integrity of the job you've done. You are the creator of your own knowingness. Yes, I would hold on to that forever.

Chapter Six

The Heart Light

I wish I had known that you could use birdseed to make your breasts look bigger and more natural. You just stuffed it into the bra and it 'conformed' to you. It moved naturally and no one could tell the difference! But who knew such things? I was finishing my role in *Jimmy the Kid* when I was told this invaluable piece of information, but it was too late. I had worked for six weeks with an overly padded, stuffed to the brim, heavy as nails bra so I could look somewhat voluptuous for the part of May that I was having so much fun playing in this silly little comedy. My small (albeit perky) breasts didn't match the airheaded blonde's 'profile,' someone who chewed bubblegum and wore big fake eyelashes.

I had gotten to work with Ruth Gordon and Paul Le Mat and was paid my largest salary to date for just having fun. Every moment was a creative mix of improvisation and scripted comedy. It takes a real connection with your fellow actors to trust them enough to do improv, but it is the secret behind the creative ride. I threw myself into this performance with abandon, and it created magic. Everything had been pretty perfect from the beginning. The negotiations were a piece of cake: I was honored with an appropriate and fair compensation, had been included in several of the creative meetings, and been invited to pre-shoot get-together dinners with the director and producers and fellow actors. I felt seen and heard and appreciated both creatively and personally. I had an absolute blast working with the hair and wardrobe people on the crazy look for this loony, wonderful character.

What added to the fun was that Chris visited me and brought

my beloved Gram Bow, who was out for her summer visit. Chris lovingly took good care of her during the long hours of shooting. He was wonderful that way. He embraced my family as his own, and took care of Gram because he loved her, not because of some sense of duty. The set photographer took some great pictures of the three of us, and Gram got to have her makeup done in 'the chair.' I could have my family on and off the set. Oh, how she loved Chris and visiting the set and cooking for us. My life was so happy and fulfilled. And then unbelievably, one call made it even better, or so I thought at the time.

I picked up the phone. It was my agent. 'Steven Spielberg wants you to star in his next film.'

I believe my response was a deadheaded 'Huh?' My agent repeated the offer. 'Oh my God!' I exclaimed. 'Oh my God.'

That was all he could tell me at the time. It was a top-secret project and he didn't have much information, only that it had something to do with an alien. And I didn't have to audition because I had gone in for his movie *Used Cars*. 'I'll call you back,' he said and hung up. Seriously, that's all I remember from one of the biggest phone calls in my life. It was sort of like getting married – it was all a blur after that first sentence. I was out by our pool having lunch with Chris and Grandma. I ran to tell them the news, and we were all screaming and clapping and whooping it up, like it was a good old Kansas rodeo. Finally, I thought, I'm in the really big time. Finally, I will make the kind of money that will let me relax and know I am secure. My impoverished childhood had subconsciously held me hostage to the fear of not having enough. This, I thought, was the break that would let me bury that fear forever.

My agent called two days later. He wanted to start negotiating this deal. Did I want to do it?

Did he think I had gone to the moon? Of course I wanted to work with Spielberg! He had leapt to instant director stardom with *Jaws* and had just done *Raiders of the Lost Ark*. Not only was he big-time, he was talented. Not only was he talented, but he was nice. I had had a beautiful meeting with him when I auditioned for *Used Cars*, and he had seemed very available and rather – well, nice.

'I'd like to read the script first,' I said.

My agent stammered. 'It's Steven Spielberg, Dee. Why do you even have to read the script?' I didn't understand. Any director would want to first know that you liked the part and could do it.

'Excuse me?' How could an actor in integrity take something she hadn't read first?

'Fine. I'll call you back.'

Why was I already in fear about doing something wrong? Minutes later he called back.

'Well?' I queried.

'The studio pretty much asked the same question,' he answered. 'And they don't want the script out to anyone.'

I was dumbfounded. But I knew that I couldn't do anything if I didn't KNOW what was expected of me. 'I have to read the script. How do I know if I connect to the material? It's for their sake as well as mine.'

A long sigh, a hang up. Another call. 'Fine, but you have to go to the studio. You can only read it behind locked doors.'

If Charles had been watching this scene, he would have instantly yelled, 'Judgment, Dee! You're going into judgment!' At the time, I thought this was pretty silly and dramatic even by Hollywood standards. In retrospect, I understand it now. Trendsetters like Spielberg and James Cameron had to be careful of copycat projects springing up. That's one reason why the initial title for *E.T.* was *A Boy's Life*.

Two days later I arrived at the studio and was escorted to a room, and read the script behind closed doors after signing away my firstborn if I breathed a word of it to anyone. It took me about two hours to read, and I remember exactly what I said when I called my agent. 'It's beautiful. It's exactly the kind of material I want to do. It's probably not going to do much for my career, but it is going to affect the world and I want to be a part of that.' It was creatively all my actor's heart had ever dreamed of doing.

And then the negotiations began. I expected them to be joyous and effortless. After all, this was a studio picture with a big director. They had money and I was still a relative peon. If my agents got me five times what I had made on my last two pictures, it would have been very meager by star standards in Hollywood dollars. I blithely went on with my life, going to class, reading other scripts. I had learned to stay out of negotiations as much as possible. They always plugged me back into my self-worth issues. I knew it was their job to get the best deal. But when they argued about what seemed to be the basic amenities that an actor needed, or money amounts that were the going rate given the body of your work and the nature of the project, I just ended up taking it personally, as did most actors. For example, you can't stay in a small room or trailer for three months, twelve hours a day, and be expected to show up on the set fresh, rested, and ready to work well. Asking for a good trailer or a dressing room isn't a star trip; it's a necessity for good work. Period.

I anticipated hearing from my agent within days. A week later, when I hadn't heard back, I called him. What the hell was going on?

'Stay out of it, Dee.' I pushed him. 'Stay out of it. You're just going to get nutty.' Again I pushed. 'Okay. The studio wants you to do it for …' Suffice it to say, a very meager sum.

'WHAT?' I exploded.

I could hear him sigh over the phone. 'We're working on it. I'll get back to you.'

I was stunned. This isn't how things were 'supposed' to work. The greater the body of your work, the greater your money. Just like they did with directors! Those integrity and fairness issues came up again. The 'Deanna Bowers isn't good enough/smart enough/her dad's an alcoholic/they're poor/we never get to the big ring' beliefs from childhood swamped me with feelings of disappointment. And here I was again, taking it personally. And that was death for me. My heart closed down for protection as my judgment of not being heard and being totally devoid of any control crept in. Because when your heart closes, the monkey-mind takes over. The litany began: They're the big guys exploiting my creativity, and I need to stand up in integrity, which probably translates into not being taken care of, so I have to fight back to be okay with myself. This was the same old script I'd run from childhood. Deanna Bowers was seven years old at the door with the money collectors again.

Two weeks later and they got the money up – a little. But it was not anywhere close to what I had made on the two little independent films I had just completed. These back-and-forth negotiations and arguments with the studio continued for six weeks. Finally, they called to say that if I didn't accept the deal, they were moving on to their second choice. I inquired who that was. It was a lovely lady, a talk show host, but she wasn't an actress. I gave them my blessings.

'Take the deal,' my agent and manager said. Wait a minute! These were the same reps who had told me to pass on *The Howling*, and to pass on the last two pics if they didn't meet my quote. Here I am, doing what they have taught me to do, and now they're caving! What the hell for?

'Why?' I demanded.

'Because it's a Steven Spielberg production with Universal Studios.'

I refused to believe that Spielberg's camp was instigating this travesty. I would later come to understand that in the 1970s and 80s big directors were the stars of Hollywood, the ones with the consistent box office. The actors, writers, even the producers in these studio films were often considered expendable. The other side of it was what it would do for your career and future earning capacity.

'That's why I SHOULDN'T do it for less. Tell them "No thank you," and that they can move on.'

Miraculously, they came back and accepted the deal. I justified my conflicting feelings with the fact that what I had asked for was fair and right. So why in the hell was I feeling guilty about it all?

My excitement about the creative side of this film had been tainted a bit during the negotiations with the studio. I was feeling slightly disrespected and devalued. I wasn't aware of taking that to the set, but in retrospect I can acknowledge that I did. Those six weeks had somehow taken me out of my knowing. I had closed my heart down during the negotiations and wasn't even aware of it. And when I closed my heart, I couldn't connect to anything but my head. It was a hellish place that I had experienced too many times in class.

'You're not connecting!' Charles would yell.

'I'm looking right at him,' I would reply in exasperation.

'But you're not connecting,' he would reiterate. 'Open your bloody heart!' I would think of one of my beloved pets. That always did it for me, my mainline to the heart. Charles could sense the difference. 'Okay, now connect that with THEM. Give it to them. See the cords of energy flowing out to them.'

I know it seems so simple, but most of us are inept at connecting up with our hearts. An example would be the waitress at your favorite coffee shop: you look at her, talk with her, ask her questions, pay her with a thank you, but do you know the color of her eyes? That is looking at someone and not creating a heart connection, an intimate moment. You're just going through the motions. It's also being in the moment to be focused on the here and now and not lost in some mental abstraction or emotional rift about past injuries.

You could be looking at your partner two inches away from you, but if you weren't connecting, it felt as if the 5:00 P.M. freeway traffic were passing between the two of you. There was no communication on a vibratory level: everything was on the surface. It became a mental moment, not a heart moment, and that's when you began manipulating the material. That was what was happening to me now in real life. I had pulled back into myself and lost my connection. And that applied, as I had insisted with Charles earlier, not only to actors but to the business people as well. I wasn't connecting to them. Interestingly enough, my life at that time was a continuing metaphor between the Universe and Universal Studios. And the scene I was manipulating was life itself. The business part had thwarted the creative part, and the left, masculine side of the brain had reared its ugly head again. Just let me be creative – that's where I'm safe. Of course, I could've been more conscious and looked at it from their point of view, but I simply didn't know how. The genetic pattern of them/us was way too ingrained in my cells.

The first day of rehearsal arrived, when we were all to meet each other and hang out, etc. Steven walked out to us and stopped cold in his tracks. 'Dee. You cut your hair.' I could see from his reaction that this was a definite no-no.

Indeed, I had cut my hair. I was used to doing independent films and TV, where you created your own look, pulled your own clothes, etc. If you were responsible, you created your look. That had actually become a step in creating the character for me. I hadn't realized that wasn't done on studio films, and that the actor needed to collaborate with the director, to make the look fit his 'vision.' It reminded me of the time I showed up on the movie 10 with my own lingerie. I should have known better. I was a working professional. But again, when you don't know something that's obvious to everybody else, it's often a subconscious attitude surfacing. I was no doubt trying to keep myself safe by exercising some control. After all, when little Deanna Bowers handled the bill collectors, everybody was safer.

In the end, the hair worked just fine, and was much easier to maintain. I was informed by the stylist that Steven had been worried about the continuity of keeping the short hair consistent. I wondered about that. Once when I was trying to figure out how to match a shot that was connecting to another shot, he instructed me not to worry. He edited too quickly. They'd never know. So somehow, I think the hair really couldn't have been a continuity issue; I think it was a guy thing about long hair. Chris wasn't too happy, either.

We all had to have security badges to get into the soundstage and onto the set. One day, three weeks into the shoot, I left mine at home. They wouldn't let me on. What the hell. This was getting stupid. My ego roared. Okay, I thought, I'll go to my room and wait.

When I say I went to my dressing room, it is an understatement. It was more like a closet, with no bathroom. I had decorated it to make it more livable, but it definitely wasn't my favorite place to hang out. After the haggle with the money, I guess my agents didn't even want to discuss a dressing room. Where was Blake Edwards when you needed him?

They finally found me. 'Dee,' the second assistant director said as he opened the door, 'I called you to the set fifteen minutes ago.'

'They won't let me on. I don't have the friggin' badge.'

'Why not?'

Well, that was a good question. I had inadvertently left it at home. So kill me.

'Come on,' he said. 'I'll walk you on.' I was feeling more and more like a kindergartner on the first day of school. I heard the next day that once they hadn't even let Steven on without a badge. I guess he didn't take it as personally. But then, he had a really cool office.

It occurred to me that I was not totally happy about how some of this 'business' was playing out. But I was gloriously happy when we were working and shooting and in the creative process. When Steven saw me do my work in the early dinner table, he actually added the bit at the sink where I turn around into the camera with that poignant line: 'He hates Mexico.' He directed me sparingly and trusted me as an actor. The kids and I were absolutely magical together. It was easy for me to open my heart with children. There was an amazing natural connection of being in the moment with all of them. Steven enhanced that by throwing out lines and directions as the camera rolled. We never knew what was coming, and it forced us to be the characters and live in the moments of their reality. That connection created natural reactions, like my spontaneous laugh at the 'penis breath' putdown, Drew's heartfelt reaction to E.T. on the operating table, and Henry's true love of an ungainly alien creature that ultimately won us all over.

Even between scenes, our heartfelt connection to E.T. carried over for all of us. We would often find Drew in the corner talking to E.T. between takes, as if he were another kid hanging out on the set. The creature was lovingly and consistently kept alive for us by dedicated special effects people, which added to the magic on the set. E.T., for all practical purposes, became another actor. When the camera rolled, it was all very magical. When I heard 'Cut,' I had to return to the business of waiting in a crummy dressing room. On the creative side, my safe place, and in my precious right brain, everything was glorious. But the money battles and my own fears had activated my mental, business side and that was death for me. For the first time in my career, I couldn't figure how to get back to my heart space off the set. I was out of trust, judgmental, and in reaction. I thought it was directed toward everyone else. Now I know it was me, fighting the battle within. The battle was staying in my power in the midst of others exercising theirs. And I was losing.

Oftentimes I would sit in that dressing room for days without ever walking onto a set. It was driving me crazy. Again, from my perspective of self-worth and victimhood, I perceived that as disrespect. They had bought me, and they could have me. And if that's your perspective, then that will be the reality you create. However, I'm not alone in this reaction to waiting around. Ask any actor. They will tell you the thing they hate the most about making movies: WAITING. You really get paid for waiting. You'd act for free. But to look at it as disrespect is something that I have to own. I finally approached Steven and complained that I had been there for three weeks and never stepped onto a set. In fact, they weren't even working on a set that I had any scenes on! He asked why that bothered me. I instantly came up with this analogy which to this day stands true: Actors are like racehorses. You pick us from the 'stable,' and we know we're going to get to run. We arrive at the 'track'; you 'groom' us, 'saddle' us, and take us to the gate. If we don't get to run, we simply want to break that damn gate down. It's true. The energy mounts until there is simply nowhere for it to go.

'Wow,' he responded, 'I never understood that. Thanks, Dee.'

The next day I was on the set again at seven, but didn't work for another three days. Why hadn't I been heard? I still stand by the principle that you shouldn't call an actor unless you need him. It's not conducive to the creative side.

But then that brings up a different perspective that I couldn't see then because I was in my 'victim' mode. I wanted the freedom to express and find my actor's moment when I was working. I didn't want to be bound by what I 'had' to do. What if Steven had had a new idea and needed to add me somewhere in a spurt of creativity? He couldn't have followed that if I had not been ready – like the end scene with the rainbow. They frantically called me in to get a shot off before lunch. I got to the set, and Steven explained about how to do the last shot when the rainbow streaks across the sky. He pointed from left to right (as in the path of the rainbow), said something about the emotional end of the movie, I heard 'Roll the camera,' and we did it. I was there. Dressed. Ready. So it happened. And then we went to lunch. Thank God for Charles and his training. Thank God for my heart always being opened when the cameras rolled. The magical connection to my heart, to the movie, to the kids, and to E.T. himself, created this amazing adventure for families through decades to come. But the roller coaster of yin/yang, heart/mind, and right brain/left brain split was making me feel like a schizophrenic child in a house of mirrors.

This was a pattern that had plagued my father: creativity versus business. He had created amazing inventions and always had inspired ideas. Yet I remember him bemoaning over and over again about how he had always been sabotaged by partners he had trusted. And I was feeling more like my dad every minute on this shoot. Was I creating the same scenarios from my expectations and genetic predisposition? And it was the business that Charles was always lamenting about – if they would just let the creative alone. The damn business end was always disconnected from the creative. Now I know that whatever your beliefs are, you will attract experiences into your life that will expose them so they can be healed. But back then such concepts were beyond me. My consciousness just hadn't moved up the frequency scale enough to understand that everything was my creation.

I can see now that I set this up as one of my biggest soul lessons. The analogy is almost funny. It's a film about being stranded, being alone, not being safe. In order to get back to his 'home,' E.T. has to trust his adopted family and the 'Universe' to get him there. His whole return journey was creative, and he went about the business of his journey in the same spirit. And he had to keep his heart light on. If only I could have understood the story that was being told: keep your heart open on the journey back to the home of your authentic self. I wasn't really following that higher direction very well.

I would anxiously look forward to the weekends when I could get back to relaxing and letting down my guard. Chris and I would go antiquing, or take Gram on studio tours. We would have glorious Sunday brunches on the patio with our two doggies, and I could curl up at night in the safe, masculine arms of my protector as I drifted off to sleep. It would've helped me if Chris could visit on the lot, but it wasn't allowed. Even that safety net wasn't available. Chris couldn't save me this time. This was a lesson I had to face on my own.

The kids always helped to anchor me. And I was very protective of them, and found myself wanting to actually 'mother' them all of the time. I especially worried about Drew. She was only four years old, and I knew at that age that the lines between reality and pretending were very blurred. So, when we came to the scene where E.T. is 'dying' on the table, I lifted her up to my lap (one of her favorite places to hang out on the set) and began to reassure her.

'So Drew,' I offered in my most nurturing voice, 'you know this scene is just pretending.'

'Uh-huh,' she replied rather matter-of-factly.

'You know E.T. isn't really hurt,' I said.

'Uh-huh.'

'You know he's acting like we do and he'll be fine when Steven yells "Cut."'

'Of course, Dee,' she answered in her very grown-up, four-year-old voice. 'I'm not stupid, you know.'

What a relief. I had done my job. I picked her up and we walked to the set. She took one look at E.T. on the operating table and totally lost it. 'He's DYING! He's DYING!' she continued to wail hysterically. So much for the line between fantasy and reality. It was another yin/yang metaphor.

I think, in retrospect, that I created my own personal *Jaws*: a shark in the waters of my life trying to attack me and take me under. I just didn't know that it was within me. What had been a magical connection to the heart of the Universe had been thwarted by my perspective that the sharks were out to get me. And I was definitely going under. The pattern that I had witnessed in my dad's life was being recreated in my own from fearful expectations that had lain dormant for so long. My naiveté finally was thwarted, and I forgot to trust the Universe because of my experience with Universal Studios. What a metaphor.

We finished the shoot and waited for post-production. One day I got a call. It was my agent. 'The studio wants you to give up your billing on E.T.'

Again. Stunned. 'Huh?' He repeated himself. 'Isn't that against Screen Actors Guild rules?' I asked.

'Yep.'

'Then why are you asking me?'

'Because it's a Steven Spielberg film. They don't want anybody else's name to appear before the film begins.' Again, the power of the studios to dictate terms and to have everybody running for cover. I was finding out just how afraid my reps were of their power.

'Look, I need to get my name known. I need to connect my name to my face. And it's against my union's rules. I can't okay that.'

'You're making a mistake,' he said. There was something almost ominous in his voice. I called my manager.

'You're making a mistake,' he said. What the hell! I was right. Those were the rules – and I was making a mistake? I didn't understand, I didn't know what to do, and I was being abandoned, I felt, by the people who were supposed to be taking care of me. Obviously, the sharks were circling them, too.

I called my mom. 'DD,' she said. 'All I can tell you is that making a decision out of fear is never the right choice.' And I knew she was right.

I sought guidance from Chris, too. After all, he was an actor. He had been challenged with his own show business demons, like a very big female casting director who tried to kill his career because he wouldn't sleep with her. 'Pupper,' he would smile at me, 'do what you think is right. I'll support you whatever decision you make.' Do what was right. The challenge was in staying clear, whether it was my ego's 'right' or my heart's 'right.' It came down to me sticking by the Actors Guild's rules. So I said no. And while the jury's still out on that decision, the fact is I didn't do another major studio film for fifteen years despite the huge success of *E.T.* It would be like Kate Winslet not doing studio films after *Titanic*.

When the film came out, I stood in line with everyone else the first day at the Cinerama Dome. Someone called a news crew and they interviewed me. Steven must have seen it, and called. I explained that I hadn't been invited to the screenings. He apologized. But my genetic sharks had severed pieces of me that I had protected for years: the fear of self-worth, of loss, of never getting 'there.' And I was so focused on those sharks now that I was eating myself alive.

Chapter Seven

Sending Heart Energy

After filming *E.T.*, I simply didn't know how to resume my career. I felt like a character in *Waiting for Godot*, a play about two men waiting for someone who never shows up. I was waiting for the release of the film, which seemed a lifetime away. I was waiting for it to start my life and to live it as I had always envisioned. I never realized that this was it, and that I had better get with the program, or the process of life itself.

Something had happened during this shoot. My natural naiveté and trust in the Universe were somehow in question now. I had closed my heart off for protection because of the wrongly perceived belief that I was not being received. But I wasn't sending that heart energy out to the world. And the Universe was saying, 'Dude! Where the hell did you go? We had such a great gig going!' But I couldn't connect to that voice anymore, and hear its sound business advice. The film opened and was an instant success. My reviews were glorious. The hype was unbelievable. But major film work wasn't forthcoming. When I inquired of my agent, he kept telling me to be patient. The work would come. It never did.

Again, my fear of never getting 'there' kept biting at my butt, and no matter how hard I tried, I was losing my drawers just as surely as the little girl in the Coppertone ads. My butt just wasn't that cute. I was frustrated. Again, it wasn't supposed to happen this way. My Midwest family taught me that if I worked hard, was responsible and did my part, I would succeed. And I bought it. They didn't know and couldn't tell me that you have to hold on to that belief, because if you change it, you change the outcome.

It had changed. It had changed because of me. I was in reaction to everything outside of me, and 'this little light of mine' decided to take a big leave of absence. I felt like I had done my job with an open heart and the business part had killed it off. So I came to the lame conclusion to shut my heart down, to insulate myself from the business part that couldn't receive it. 'Hello!' the Universe called out. 'It's show BUSINESS!' But I couldn't hear it. This belief was already too big to let that voice resonate.

So I was waiting, and I'm not good at waiting. Remember the card from my mother with the vultures? It brought up an interesting dichotomy now. Yes, patience in allowing the perfection of the Universe to manifest is good. Waiting for a film to save you and define you – not so great. I somehow needed to keep creating. That was where I was safe. That was where I was in my joy. But no one was hiring me to act. I didn't know then that it wasn't about them. Creation was up to me! I had given that power away. *E.T.* was the biggest blockbuster of all time. Producers would call all excited about hiring me for their next project, and days later they just 'changed their mind.' I remember a great little film called *Starman*. I had met with the producers and read for the part, and they were quite enthusiastic about my coming onboard. And then, poof! – it was gone in sixty seconds. They went with Karen Allen whose last big film had been *Raiders of the Lost Ark* – she gave a wonderful performance. Everyone gave me this song-and-dance routine that perhaps I shouldn't do another sci-fi film right after *E.T.* Hmm. It's usually actors who want to switch genres and not get typecast, not producers and studios. It didn't make any sense. So it pointed to THEM. Damn those sharks.

Thank God for Chris. Again. He was much more into this 'you create your own reality' philosophy at the time. 'Just hold steady,' he would say. 'Just be happy, Pupper.' But I couldn't be happy and know who I was without a career to help me define myself. So that definition became: an actress who wasn't working at a certain level!

Maybe Chris's spiritual 'distance' came from his out-of-body experience. Before I met him, he had had a brain aneurism. They didn't think he would make it overnight. My big marine would tell the story of how he left his body and hung out up in the corner of the ceiling. He turned and saw the tunnel and light, and would speak lovingly and longingly about the peace and knowing he felt in that moment. He started to go into the light, turned back for a last look at his family around him, had a quick thought about 'there is something more I'm supposed to do' and BAM, he was back in his body. He came away with a knowing that all was one, and good, and simply to be enjoyed. He was never afraid of dying, he said. Chris had seen the other side, and it was pure love. I longed to really know in my being that experience of a higher love, but right now I was still consumed with fear.

And then Dan Blatt called. He was getting ready to do a Stephen King novel about a rabid Saint Bernard that was keeping a woman and her son hostage in a Pinto for days without water in suffocating heat. I am sure you can see the analogy already. The Universe, if nothing else, often has a weird sense of humor when showing us the obvious: an ominous, uncontrollable force is keeping me from moving and surviving, threatening my family, and I am powerless to defend myself. Wow. We all have an amazing mechanism for turning belief into reality and, in my case, quickly in the form of a movie. But this time it wasn't 'only a movie.' This time the movie was my life.

So what does an actress do when she's scared and confused? I went back to class. While I had been gone, Charles had decided to change his teaching style a bit. We were now not allowed to read the scene even once before we performed it.

I didn't like this approach. I liked reading it once 'to get the lay of the land.' I mean, if it ain't broke, don't fix it. I felt that the subconscious needed some direction, just like an actor. Even my trusted acting technique was being thwarted.

'I don't get it,' I said to him before class. 'What exactly is the point?'

'The point is to not let your friggin' mind have the slightest chance to get involved.' There was that famous Charles tone again. I trusted him. I committed to play the new game. When I finished the scene, I waited as usual for my master's voice. 'Well,' he asked, 'don't you love working this way?'

I didn't. But knowing I was being 'shown off', and wanting to support my hero, I stammered something about needing to work with it more and it was interesting … blah, blah, blah. But when I left that day, I knew that my Camelot acting studio was undergoing change, and that this alteration of the technique only served to make me more unstable. I decided to keep to my trusted formula. And besides, I had a movie offer on the table.

I read the script. It was a tour de force role. It was the kind of emotional ride that I loved, and I identified with the quest of the mother saving her child. Interesting that I was attracting all these mother roles before I had a child of my own. But I deeply knew those mothers: I had been raised by one who selflessly gave herself in defending and nurturing her children against all odds. And I innately had compassion for animals and all helpless energy that needed protection. There was just one problem: a graphic naked love scene.

I called Dan. 'I love this. I want to do this. But I don't think I can …'

He cut me off. 'There won't be any nudity.'

That was easy. 'I don't know about the …'

He cut me off again. 'We want Chris to play your lover.'

Well, hell's bells; it just doesn't get any easier than that. And he doubled my salary from *E.T.* We had a motor home for our dressing room. I was received. Chris and I moved into this beautiful home in northern California overlooking a deep valley where hot-air balloonists sailed on weekly outings. I would need this refuge. I was about to embark on the most emotionally difficult, physically demanding acting job I would ever tackle.

They picked me up at five every morning, and I rarely got home before eight at night. One time our friends came up to visit and we went to dinner. I fell asleep at the table. But it was glorious. It demanded a constant heart connection between Danny Pintauro, my four-year-old co-star, and me. That's the great thing about working with kids – and dogs for that matter. Their hearts are always open to connect with yours. You don't consciously have to choose to keep yours open. I was blessed to have this amazing young actor to share this journey. I wanted to connect with the dogs, too. I love animals, and have worked with many rescue charities. But we weren't allowed to connect. It wasn't good for the dogs to be personally bonded with anyone but the trainer, I was told. I understood that, but it was difficult and sad for me. Karl Miller, our animal trainer, empathized with me, but didn't give in. Karl was such a gentle giant, and had those dogs trained to perfection. You could see the immense love he had for them. He even slept with them in the barn. I told Chris about my dilemma and how I missed our beloved Spirit, who had stayed at home so he wouldn't be traumatized. The next day I came home and was greeted by my four-legged friend at the door. Chris had a friend drive him up from LA. Yes. My heart connection was always received by Chris. I was greatly honored, loved, and taken care of by my soul mate.

The first director on *Cujo* was an Englishman named Peter Medak, who had done an amazing film called *The Ruling Class* with Peter O'Toole. I was excited about being directed by someone with his creativity, but had not met with him until I arrived in northern California two weeks prior to filming. During wardrobe discussions, we began running into problems. He had a vision of my character wearing transparent gauzy clothing that you could see through … without a bra. It just took the picture in the wrong direction, placing the focus on the affair and not the mother/child bond. Donna needed to be sympathetic so the audience would root for her victory over the canine and its destructive forces. I'm a mother defending her child. I'd have to get filthy and sweaty and be bloodied. He thought I could just get sexier and sexier as the clothes came off. But that was simply wrong for the character. We had a meeting with Dan. 'What the hell are you talking about?' Dan asked him. I was wondering what had been discussed in the production meetings that they were supposed to have had. Peter conceded the point. Other differing points were worked out. Filming began. In the first two days, it became apparent that we were doing two versions of the same movie. Everything about the dog was a sexual metaphor. Everything about the mother/child relationship seemed to have those same undertones. Dan and I looked at the first day's dailies. They just didn't work. I looked at my producer.

'What do you think, Dee?' he asked. I remember tearing up at the sheer experience of being treated as an equal in that moment. A comrade. A creative partner. Dan put his hand on my arm. 'What is it, Dee?' I shared my feelings. 'Well, you are. I respect your opinion. What do you think?'

'I think he's shooting a different film than what we envisioned. It's all very creative, very interesting. But it's not the gritty, down-and-dirty film we set out to make.'

He paused for a moment. 'I agree,' he sighed. 'We have to follow our original instinct and trust it.'

It was so easy to trust with Dan. He received me. Ultimately, it was his decision, but I expressed my feelings. It is interesting that when an actor does come forward to state his or her opinion in support of a better product or a clearer vision, he or she is often branded as 'difficult' or 'not being a team player.' It's usually the opposite: we care so much that we want to be an integral part of the creative vision.

Within three days Peter was out, replaced by a man named Lewis Teague. Dan had originally talked to Lewis some time earlier, and he had done some preliminary work on the film.

Lewis was kind, gentle, and had a true vision and unending patience. He brought a balance and grace to a set that could have been difficult and volatile simply because of the emotional demands on everyone. He also worked well with our brilliant director of photography, Jan de Bont. Jan was a genius at coming up with creative shot angles that kept what could have been a static presentation very active and alive, and moving forward during the last hour when we were stranded in the car. (He later showed this same brilliance when directing the thriller *Speed* with Sandra Bullock.) Somehow, we all connected and everything jelled – the kid, the dogs, the director, the cinematographer, the actors, and even the weather.

We were under the gun. It was October going into November in northern California. The rains were coming. We were working on a real farm, and rain was our greatest nemesis. I was so exhausted after the car sequences that Dan had promised me a week off to bounce back. But he simply couldn't give it to me. The weather was moving in on us. Most days we were all freezing. They even had to put a heater in the front of the car because Danny and I would get so cold that we couldn't stop shaking. Having the shivers when you are supposed to be dying of heat just doesn't work.

There were hundreds of little challenges every day. For instance, the dogs were trained to go after toys, and Karl would yell 'Dig! Dig for that toy!' and the dog of choice that day (there were five in total) would launch into a frenzy of clawing and barking and jumping for the toy. From the waist up, the dog looked like he could eat you alive. We quickly discovered in dailies, however, that they were wagging their tails in delightful anticipation of getting their prize. Ultimately we gently tied their waggers down with fish wire so you couldn't see their glee. And then there were the egg whites to create the foaming-at-the-mouth effect. They licked so many egg whites that I'm surprised their cholesterol didn't jump. Danny and I and the entire crew would have to be ready to go because as soon as the egg whites were placed on the dogs, we immediately had to dive into the action before their tongues consumed the frothy mixture. It was kind of like acting with a pistol start. And I had to always be committed and in the moment, because when the kid and the dog worked at the same time, you'd better believe they printed the take.

And I loved it all. It was so easy for me to harmoniously meld the business and the creative together on *Cujo*. Because I was taken care of, it was easy to keep my heart light on and connect to the energy around me. Charles would beat this into us: looking is not seeing, planning is not seeing, only sending your energy to your partner is truly seeing them. It is the connection of your energy to them that creates the harmonious and truthful response back from them. It is, literally, intentionally sending your energy over into a completion of the connection. I now know that the secret for me is being allowed to connect. If I feel that I am being shut out, I usually react and stop creating, and forget that it's my choice and I can choose to continue. This is precisely what had happened during the process of making *E.T.* The truth is that there is nothing that can keep you from opening yourself and making that connection. No one but you. But most of us don't know that. And those of us that do often won't take the responsibility that the buck stops with us. So I was relying on outside circumstances to dictate my own heart. I was definitely out of choice.

I had started pointing the finger at them – whoever the hell they were – because it didn't make sense that I was sabotaging myself. Ah, if I only knew then what I know now.

So, as I was filming a movie about a 200-pound dog that was out to kill me, I was creating a 200-pound gorilla in the imaginary perception of my psyche. And neither one of them was real. The rabid dog was really five gentle, furry teddy bears, and the gorilla was a windmill in my mind. The only thing they had in common was fear. Illusory fear. The basis of all horror films – in the movies and in life. It hasn't escaped me that my many horror films express a subconscious need early in life to master fear or that monster within me. It is clear that my entire life journey has been a quest to find that 'little light of mine' again and keep it emanating. To be safe being me. If I was unclear about doing that in life, I was certainly attracting work in a genre of films where I had to face my demons snout on. And right now, the demon was 'them.'

I was disconnecting from the very energy I wanted to be a part of. I was brilliantly creating this 'me/them' scenario. Charles had taught us this lesson – and at times by his own example – but I had conveniently forgotten that it applied to life. Like the new partner I had judged in class, I was judging the people in the business. Hell, I was judging the business, period. And I had created a separation that wouldn't allow me to connect and send out the very energy that creates manifestation. No wonder the calls weren't coming in. The perception of what we see is usually, like the dog in *Cujo*, not real. But we allow ourselves to make it real, and then our life does, really, get created that way. But the Universe keeps giving us clues that we are on the wrong track.

And it also tells us when we are heading in the right direction. The day came to shoot the big seizure scene where my son becomes traumatized due to dehydration. I was concerned about Danny. Again I worried about those blurry lines between reality and fantasy with child actors. In retrospect, he seems to have had a better handle on it than I did.

'I've had one of those, Dee. I know what to do. You wanna see one?' I nodded my head. 'See, my head goes back kinda like this and my eyes kinda roll like this, and I grab my throat like this,' he said, clutching his throat, 'and …'

'That's great, Danny. But let's save it for the scene,' I said, not wanting him to over-rehearse it.

We headed back to the old Pinto, got in, and they spent a few minutes checking the light and setting up the shot. And then the camera rolled, and I went into emotional Lalaland, and Danny went into his seizure, while the dog went into his toy mania. The sounds of the boy's wheezing breath and the dog's growling nearly sent me over the edge. And then Danny started screaming, 'I want my dad! I want my dad!' And before I knew it, I had grabbed him by the shoulders and was yelling angrily, 'All right, I'LL GET YOU YOUR FATHER.' It is the most realistic moment in the film: a moment every parent knows, when you are in such fear for your beloved child that you lose it emotionally. And I did. In that moment my heart was wide open and responding from some deep vein of parental reaction.

Dan came to me the next day. The footage, he said, was amazing. He had one concern: maybe my reaction was too frightening – too, well, real. He didn't want the audience to lose their sympathy for the character. I blinked my eyes. 'Every parent everywhere in the world will identify with that reaction,' I told him. 'Let's have the balls to go with it.' We did, and it was the most talked about of all the scenes in the whole movie. It was also a prime example of why this was the most physically demanding role I have ever played.

While shooting *Cujo*, I blew out my adrenals, which are your fight-or-flight control. When you are in constant fight or flight from danger, real or imaginary, your adrenals get depleted. Let's face it. We are all running from something, be it a dog or an idea. I also contracted the Coxsackie virus. It is, literally, hoof and mouth disease. I want to insert here the energetic meaning for people who get that virus. This is from *Messages from the Body*:

> They are manifesting high-stress vulnerability, due to emotional exhaustion connected with an intensely accelerated and deep-reaching healing process ... This includes re-contacting very deep emotional wounds and early deprivations and degradations, with a surfacing and releasing of

long-suppressed grief and mourning. It also involves revamping their entire belief system ... It is indicative of significant progress toward liberation from the patterns that are being cleared out.

I guess my healing had begun, but I mean really, how much louder can the Universe be screaming at me? 'Dee! Stop running. Start creating! Start connecting that heart light again.' But did Dee listen? Hell no. Dee was being too much of a victim to hear.

Thank God I had Chris, who was my balance in this storm. He would look for ways to pick me up and keep life lighter. One day we were on our way to the farm for the day's shoot. We turned the bend and there must have been a hundred sheep standing in the road staring at us.

'Oh my God,' I said. 'What do we do?' We honked. Obviously, the sheep were deaf. Chris sat there, and then broke into a hysterical laugh. 'What?' I demanded. 'I'm gonna be late.' I would have gotten more irate, except my macho marine was now falling down on the seat in uncontrollable glee.

'Get out,' he commanded.

'What?' I asked, almost in exasperation.

'Get *out*.' I did. We stood by the side of the car. 'Put your hands up.' He went into a stance as if he were being held at gunpoint. 'Put your hands up!' I did, looking at him questioningly. 'Didn't you hear them?' he asked. And, in his best alpha-sheep voice he said, 'Get out and give me all your sweaters!' It took me a brief moment to 'get it,' and then I slugged him. Soon we were rolling in the grass in hysterical laughter like two kids on a hot summer day. We scared the darn sheep so badly they ran off.

There were other humorous diversions. One of our wonderful stuntmen, Gary, helped keep me balanced whenever he could. I would be between distraught, hysterical scenes, sitting on the set with my head between my hands, and I would hear, 'Pssst.' And then a second, louder 'Pssst.' I'd look up and Gary would be in full dog regalia. Knowing how much I hated that damn Pinto by then, he would walk over, lift his leg, and mime a disgusting release of dog urine all over the piece of junk. It was a welcome relief from the emotional drama of the shoot.

The experience of my life was becoming a yo-yo of good/bad, successful/sabotaged. I remember the quintessential moment when all my fears about money should have been wiped from my slate, but they weren't. I came home from a very long day of shooting to find Chris anxiously waiting for me at the door. 'Pupper,' he said, taking me into his arms, 'guess what? I just got the news. We made half a million this year.' I should have fallen over in relief and joy, broken open the champagne, and tied one on. But my first thought was, That's too much. I don't think I ever shared that with Chris. I'm not sure I even acknowledged it myself. And I never made that much money again. Somewhere there was a little shark swimming around in my self-worth drudge, sabotaging the very thing I was trying to create. I had created it, nonetheless, but the hit I took that day began recreating my creation. I guess I was disconnected from and judging people who had money, too. The psyche is a confusing little sucker. I wonder now, in my knowingness, if that had been at the core of the negotiations during *E.T.* That experience made me come forward to claim my worth. This information made me limit it. The Universe had to be confused. I sure as hell was! All of this emotional stress combined with the physical demands of the shoot totally depleted me. Afterward I was treated for exhaustion for three weeks.

While completing the filming of *Cujo,* my agent called with the news that I had been invited to attend a royal showing of *E.T.* in London and meet the Royal Family. Dan tried to let me go, but he just couldn't risk the weather turning on us. It was a great disappointment to me. It would have been a lovely experience. But the weather had already started turning in my life. I had called the rain clouds in, and my creation was manifesting its results perfectly. There was a pattern emerging in my life, but I had to get to the sunny side of the hill to look back and see it: I had sent my energy out to connect, and it wasn't received, and so I shut down for protection and didn't send out my heart energy for a very long time. No one could respond to something they weren't receiving. And if I wasn't received, my heart light stayed out. It was, indeed, the perfect energetic storm.

Chapter Eight

The Immaculate Reception

If I was creating a perfect storm in my life, my port was acting class. I could dock there, tie up, hold steady, and weather the storm. There I could give and be received, both personally and professionally. Personally it was a given. But there was also a technique for doing that as an actor.

If you were on the receiving end, you had to receive openly, honestly, and detached from your ego's place of safety and limited perceptions. If you felt enraged, emotional, hysterical, defensive, or even giddy, you had to run to that specific emotion without question in response to what was being given to you, and immediately send it back to your partner. That discipline of non-judgment before the response is given was what made the actors in the Studio fresh and new and daring – and REAL. It was raw truth. I liked living in raw truth.

Charles would often interrupt scenes to teach this invaluable lesson. Actors hate to be interrupted. It screws up your flow. But he made it so obvious that we forgave him the breach of etiquette.

'Did you see that?' he would yell in excitement, pointing his finger at the guilty party. 'She changed her initial response. She had a truthful, immediate response, and she screwed it up with a fucking idea about what's okay.' He was right. We all could see it. The mind would get in the way quicker than any of us could fathom. 'It's not about what is right. It's about what is real!'

I wanted it to be that way in life. I wanted everything to be real from that heart place. I didn't want everyone trying to manipulate me, because in response my mind became manipulative from the sheer challenge of trying to stay safe.

But there was a dangerous reinforcement happening in class between Charles and me. For the first time, I needed an ally for my victimhood: someone to share in the negativity of what I perceived as wrongdoing against me. I needed someone to tell me unconditionally what I knew in my heart was false – that the world was now against Deanna Bowers. It had to be. Just like it had sabotaged Daddy.

For over a year now, I hadn't done a film. Yes, there were TV parts – some really good roles – but no films. The parts kept coming to me, and then going away. I was the same talented actress. I wasn't DOING anything different. So it must be them. I kept changing agents in the hope that someone would save me, but I just wasn't changing my core beliefs. And what you see, as they say, is what you get. I was seeing myself being sabotaged, and creating that perfectly. Charles was ready and willing to encourage my paranoia. Those assholes out there were the sharks, and all the talented peons were the food they consumed. We became comrades. It didn't serve me, or him.

Looking back on those years, it is clear that the Universe was directing me away from one closed door and giving me a chance to walk into an open one: television. But I wasn't about to receive the gift. I was doing some amazing movie-of-the-week and guest-star appearances, and some low-budget films. But I wasn't doing big, studio films with other major actors in movies that affected the world. And that is all I had ever really wanted to do. That had been my guiding intention since I watched *Gone with the Wind* and actors like Katharine Hepburn and Spencer Tracy, and my daddy would look at me and say, 'You can do that, Button-nose.' I had just always wanted to do film … period.

So instead of guiding me into healing and moving on with life, my beloved Charles joined me in falling deeper into the mire. Like your friend in grade school, everything was more permissible if you had a cohort to get in trouble with. Together we joined in energetically targeting the business end of Hollywood and creating them as adversaries. It made me angry. It made me unhappy. But it felt righteous.

I was sabotaging myself at every turn. NBC had come to me and I had met with Brandon Tartikoff, the president of NBC. 'We love your work, Dee. We loved you in *E.T.* We'd love to have you here at NBC. We can get you a gig on *Saturday Night Live*, and we'd love to find a series for you to star in.'

Sure, I thought, because you can have the actress from the biggest blockbuster of all time on TV! I am embarrassed to share that, but it's how I felt then. Talk about looking a gift horse in the mouth. The Universe was leading me to water, but I'd be damned if I was going to take a drink.

They brought me a series produced by a kind and wonderful man who was an enormous fan of my work. It was a sweet project, but it was TV. We started the negotiations. Each time we almost had a deal, I asked for something more or different, and they gave it to me. More money, more vacation, more dressing room, more money, more money … We got up to more than a million for the first year; I sent my manager back to ask for some other stupid thing, and they pulled the deal. Obviously, I had no real intention of doing this. I took a slight hit, but ultimately was relieved. I had never become an actor for the money. I had become an actor so I could move people like my mother did and change lives. In films. I didn't know the two could come together.

Chris lovingly pointed out the dichotomy of what was happening: 'You feel dishonored because you weren't given things, and now you don't honor yourself by accepting anything else. Nothing fits into your idea of how you think it should look.' It was always so simple for him. 'I love you, Pupper. I'll back you up. But you need to see the imbalance and confusion of how this is playing out.' I didn't. I had to be right. My life – and ego – depended on it.

Thank God Christmas was coming. I lived for Christmas. No matter how meager our finances, how stressful the business, or how challenged my balance of life and career had become, Christmas always brought me back to the joy of me. My family always made it important to get together. We usually traveled back to Kansas to be with Mom, but this year we had chosen to go to Bucks County, north of Philadelphia, where my older brother and soul mate, Denny, lived with his family. There was often snow on the ground and wood fires and plenty of laughter, and secret shopping outings to get last-minute presents. Wine and hot toddies were plentiful. And the outside world and its concerns came to a standstill for seven glorious days of celebration.

Denny and Chris and I went on long shopping trips so we could grab time and talk. But this particular year, I needed Denny to help me find something special for Chris. I had bought him some beautiful clothes and a book he had asked about, but not that special gift that we always had for each other and saved until the last to take a picture of the precious present being opened.

'Think out of the box, peewee. Special doesn't have to mean spending money,' my smart big brother advised.

Hmm, I thought, I do know one thing he has always wanted that I said I'd never give him.

Chris had intimated for years that he wanted me to add his name to my professional name and my personal identification. He wasn't talking about his legal name – Bourassa – which was hard to pronounce and even he had replaced. But he wanted me to add Stone, his mother's maiden name, to mine. I was Chris's girl in every way and he wanted to be sure that everyone knew it! And so for Christmas, because I wanted so much to make him happy, I became Dee Wallace Stone. No hyphen. I was so connected to him in that moment that I forgot to take the picture of him opening the small box with my Screen Actors Guild card enclosed that had the name 'Stone' added quite artistically with a marker. I just wish I had a picture of his smiling, teary-eyed face. It was a moment. But for the next four years, the consistent question from the press was about my name change: 'Are you Dee Wallace or Dee Wallace Stone?' I wanted to yell back that I was Deanna Bowers from Kansas. It was just another way my higher self was asking me to look at my own confusion. I had, figuratively and literally, become genuinely confused about who I was. And I was wondering why the Universe couldn't find me. Hell, the postman was even confused. At one point we had mail arriving for Dee Wallace, Dee Wallace Stone, Deanna Wallace, Christopher Stone, Thomas Bourassa, and Deanna Bourassa. That should have been a clue right there! At one point the mailman knocked on the door and asked, 'How many people live here, anyway?'

The Universe kept telling me that the interior created the exterior manifestation, but I still wasn't getting the lesson. 'Don't tell me I'm creating this bullshit in my life,' I said at one point to my spiritual teacher. 'I want to be a film star.' The film that I did do was another one about hairy alien creatures, called Critters, who come onto our farm and threaten to kill my family and me. Again, what a metaphor! The movie *Critters* was a lot of fun, albeit not, again, the life-affecting project I wanted to do. The best thing that came out of it was meeting a great kid named Scott Grimes.

The call came on a Friday. I had a meeting for a series that was already picked up. It was called *Together We Stand*, and I would be the mother of one natural child, a boy, one adopted daughter, and then two more adoptees that would 'fall into my life' – a little black girl and an Asian boy. I still didn't want to do a television series, but by this time we had bought a house with a swimming pool, two cars, and had our share of credit card debt – well, suffice it to say that we both had to keep pretty busy to support ourselves in the manner we had become accustomed to. I needed to receive some money. I took the meeting.

It was at Universal Studios, so I had to choose to get past that energetic block from *E.T.* at the start. It helped that film and TV negotiations were completely separate. I arrived at the office of Al Burton, a wiry, happy fifty-something man who reminded me of one of Santa's elves. It was love at first sight. Then Sherwood Schwartz stepped into the office. Sherwood was the creator of *Gilligan's Island* and was another teddy bear, a slightly older nurturing type who energetically reminded me of my favorite grandfather.

For two hours we talked and ate and laughed and discussed the project. They won me over as surely as Chris had that first dinner at Le Petit Chateau. I took the pilot script home to read. It was a sitcom, and for years Chris had chided me about needing more humor in life. We had this ongoing exchange that we lovingly shared: 'Pupper, where's your sense of humor?' he would ask.

'You know I never had one,' I would reply. It was another way we said 'I love you.' So I read the script and fell in love with it. So did Chris. 'But I haven't done much comedy,' I worried.

He countered with humor. 'This is real-life stuff. And they even have a dog. You'll be fine.'

I did resonate with the script though. It was that secondary theme that I knew so well: taking care of and protecting children. Chris and I had been trying to have a baby, with no success. That was a void in my life. Maybe pretending with a screen family could fill it. Michael Jacobs, a brilliant new writer and producer, had been hired, also. And I loved him. I loved his writing and his ideas, and I loved how he always stood up to the suits. He was brilliant. And then I met Will Mackenzie. He had been hired to direct all the episodes. Charming, sexy, funny, brilliant, nurturing. If we both hadn't been happily married, that might have gone other places. We kept it in that incredible loving, working arena where creativity soars. I was starring with Elliott Gould. The money was great. I had an on-lot dressing room just twenty minutes away from home. I was in.

During the first four episodes, I felt I had died and gone to heaven. I couldn't wait to get to the studio. I loved the scripts and the subjects we bravely tackled, like 'Is God Dead?' Do you know how much genius it takes for a writer to do that subject as a sitcom script? Yes, we were doing material that would affect people and let them laugh at the same time. In the 'Is God Dead?' episode, our daughter's school was exploring the cover story from *Time* magazine. We humorously – and philosophically – explored the different thinking and arguments around this subject, which was topical in the late 1980s. A political sitcom – who would've guessed?

But the main focus was exploring human differences through the children's ethnicities. We delved into real family issues like sex and equality. There was one particular episode about me being in fear that I couldn't be a good mother to this diverse assortment of kids. What did I know about Black or Asian history? One of the most memorable scenes was between Elliott and me. Michael Jacobs brilliantly tackled these issues – kindled in many of the viewers' homes because of the new adoption regulations – by having my character wake up from a nightmare about … bread. I was fixing everyone WHITE BREAD sandwiches, metaphorically representing who I was (as a character and Dee as a person). I was horrified that I didn't know what to serve Chairman Mao and Martin Luther King. 'All I know about Reverend King is that he had a good dream and I didn't. And then he turned into white bread, as did Chairman Mao! Everyone was white bread!'

'I was white bread?' Elliott's character inquires.

'No, silly. You were rye bread,' I say, alluding to his Jewish heritage. 'I don't want to teach these children MY heritage. They have their own.'

It was one of many touching, educational, and expansive subjects delightfully delivered in clever comedy dialogue. I was proud to be part of everything we presented in those early episodes.

I loved the kids; all of them were sweet and talented and unspoiled. I am happy to say I was instrumental in bringing Scott Grimes, whom I had met on the set of *Critters*, on board as my biological son. I will always feel good that I helped bring this great talent to the forefront.

The casting of my husband was the only glitch in what seemed to be an effortless start. We had seen close to two hundred people, and taken several of them to the network for final approval. None of them got picked. Finally, the night before we were to begin production, supposedly the studio called to give Al the ultimatum: use Elliott Gould or you don't do the show. Or so the story goes.

You've got to hate politics when it gets in the way of creativity. And I did. Don't get me wrong. I love Elliott. He is sweet and endearing, a wonderful actor, and was fabulous with the children and me. There just might have been other actors better suited to play an ex-jock who had coached basketball. But hire Elliott they did, and the next day we began our first table read. It was the pilot episode that explained how all these kids came to live under one roof with these parents, and how they opened their hearts to them. When it aired, it was selected as the best new pilot of that year.

I waited in anticipation for each new script. It was always a perfect mixture of endearing humor, heart, and message. The kids and Elliott and I became a family ourselves, along with our beloved Al and Sherwood. Again, I had attracted Camelot into my life. But, around the fourth week, I began to sense some tension on the set. No! Don't let this happen again, I thought to myself. I'm so happy. But the temporary peace between Will and the network suits was breaking down, as was the good energy between Michael and Sherwood. It's interesting, in retrospect, that even though I didn't seem to create this situation from any apparent action of my own, the repeating pattern of 'it's good and then goes away' was being replayed. I did still own that belief, and it had attracted yet another similar scenario into my life.

By the sixth episode, I was told that both Will Mackenzie, my director, and Michael Jacobs, my brilliant writer/producer, were leaving. I was devastated. The family worked! Why were we getting divorced? It appeared that Will and the studio/network couldn't come to terms on his deal and that they were making it extremely hard for him to do his job. The money issue was again in play. I think the discord with Michael was a generation gap with his elder associates. I mean, there's a pretty big creative jump between *Gilligan* and 'Is God Dead?' I loved them all. And most of all I loved them together. Damn.

Again, my Camelot was crumbling and I was helpless to save it. All I could do was to pick up the sword and try to lead my people to victory. I tried to stay positive. I choreographed a little thank you/goodbye musical number that we all performed for Will. I told the kids that we would be fine. I told Elliott I knew they'd get someone just as good. But as I was telling them, I was trying to believe it myself. I was doing a little better at receiving what I was given and 'saying it was good.' But in reality, it was hopeful lip service. I was really on the defensive and waiting to be tackled again. And I was.

We did a few more shows with several different writers, none of whom were terribly innovative. And then I got a call from my agent that really sent me reeling. The studio had decided that Elliott's character wasn't 'working' in the show. He would have to die somehow, and the family would have to go on. Now there's comedy material! Would I be willing to take a few weeks off – without pay – while they revamped the show? My talent agency had put together many of the elements of the show and 'packaged' them, including Elliott and me. Hmm. Do you think my agents then were looking out for my best interest financially during this shutdown?

But again, it was close to the holidays, and this would enable me to go back and spend more time with my family to regroup.

We would now have two weeks to visit everyone. I needed a physical break, too. Although the hours on a sitcom weren't grueling, it still took a consistent output of energy. We took off for Kansas City and what would be the last Christmas Mommy would host. I went back to my childhood home and walked into memories of my high school years: cheerleading and homecomings. There were also memories of Daddy and his fight with alcoholism, and the brave mother that brought us all through it. I was filled with gratitude and love and appreciation for her strength – and mine. Everyone came back and we lovingly put up 'Tiny Town' – a miniature city with cotton for snow and Christmas lights in the little houses, and streets full of dogs and carolers. It was a Mommy tradition, and one I still carry on today. She reminded me of the true meaning of gratitude.

During this time, I reflected on how wonderful the start-up of this series had gone. It had given me so many creative opportunities within the television format that I had always fought so vigilantly against doing. One of my greatest blessings on the show was having my mom make an appearance in a tiny cameo. It had been her life's dream to own a Screen Actors Guild card so she would be a 'legitimate' professional actor. I can't express how my heart celebrated being able to do that for her. We took pictures of her with the cast; the local newspapers interviewed her. She was in her glory. It was so little to do for this amazing woman who had initially shown me the power of touching people's hearts through acting. She had raised me by sheer willpower in the face of all odds, and had always loved me unconditionally. And she stole the scene, just like a veteran actor. I'll never forget how loving and nurturing Elliott was with her. I'll always love him for that.

So Christmas passed, spent largely in getting rebalanced and deflecting inquiries regarding the baby issue. We would just smile and say, 'It's fun trying.' But it was getting harder to pretend. I thought of all those movies where you got pregnant by accident when you didn't want to. I WANTED to – and nothing was happening. We were on our third or fourth year of dedicated baby making. Endless tests and cups of bodily fluids and fertility timing and legs up in stirrups and vaginal probes and more doctor visits. It got to the point where I would put a calendar up and circle the highest probability dates, so we could pretend it was all spontaneous for my somewhat humiliated husband. It was kind of funny in retrospect: this sexy Hollywood couple struggling to conceive a child. More than once I sent him off to the clinic with a dirty self-shot video in hopes of a successful plastic cup experience. Really romantic.

I remember visiting a very big specialist who looked me straight in the eyes and said, 'I'm sorry, Dee. In my opinion you'll never get pregnant.' Chris audibly sighed and put his head in his hands. 'I'm sorry, Mr Stone.'

Chris looked up, blinked, and said, 'No, you got it wrong, doc. You should've never told her that. She's relentless.' He was right. And I knew. I knew that God and I were going to make that baby. I knew it was going to be a girl. And I knew she would change my life.

But right now I had a show to get up and going. I was called to a meeting at Universal Studios. During the Christmas break, this is what had developed: Elliott was off the show, two new women writers had been hired, a new neighbor had been written in, and the name of the show was now *Nothing Is Easy*. Am I a good creator or what? Again, if I had only been able to understand the language of self-creation. 'Dee, hellooooo! Wake up and see the pattern here. Camelot to shit, over and over again in your life! Dude, it doesn't take a rocket scientist to realize you need to let go of whatever belief keeps creating these disasters.' But I just couldn't see the pattern: I would open my heart, give of myself, receive; then something negative would happen, and I'd react, shut my heart off, and stop receiving. Or receive what I didn't want. But alas, that awareness was still farther down my yellow brick road of consciousness.

Again I was in reaction. Again I went into fight or flight. I pulled back, went into judgment, shut my heart down, and began fighting the process. Nothing was the way it had been, including me. These weren't the scripts I signed up to do; this wasn't the energy that attracted my participation. We had gone from 'Is God Dead?' to 'Your neighbor is angry, the kids are pissed off, and the statement is: that's the way it is.' All the heart was gone. The life statements were gone. I had a meeting with the new writers at my producer's suggestion. I told them my concerns about the message and the heart and the essence of the original show. Their reply was something like 'Why would you want a sitcom that does THAT?' I rest my case. All the comedy now came from anger and sarcasm. Now I know that this was again a reflection of my own anger and resentment coming out. As within, so without, as we now say. The dichotomy of Dee! It was as if half of Dee was joyful with an open heart, and the other half was an angry victim. My life was a complete game of emotional ping-pong: receive – push away; receive – push away. And it was exhausting. Again, instead of calling it good and receiving what I was given, so I could work with it and creatively turn it around, I flipped them off and ran away. I hadn't learned Charles' lesson about receiving openly, and if my reaction was anger, I couldn't return a pure response. I had closed my heart light off, and the creative process stopped for me.

The series lasted a few more episodes and died. I ached for the beautiful kids I worked with, and the producers I loved. We were, in every sense of the word, a family. Indeed, it had literally gone from *Together We Stand* to *Nothing Is Easy*, from positive and embracing to negative and excluding, from a full circle of giving and receiving to blocking and dying. Again I was choosing not to resonate with the vibration of what I wanted, but fell into the reactionary focus of what I had lost and didn't have. And it was THEIR fault. Thank God poor little Deanna wasn't responsible.

Chapter Nine

The Zero Point

I was pretty much down to zero. The negative kind. Nothing left. Most people would look at my life and say everything was pretty darn good. From my perspective, I just couldn't see it that way. I didn't consider them blessings, in disguise or otherwise, unless they were exactly what I wanted. And I wasn't doing films or creating a baby, so nothing was a blessing. Boy, did I need a wake-up call.

That came as an offer to do a movie in Australia with a director named George Miller. He had done a wonderful film that I loved called *The Man from Snowy River*. And I got excited. It was a period piece – and it was about Christmas. If there was one subject that could open my heart other than kids, animals, and Chris, it was Christmas. As I've said, Christmas has always brought my family together in a huge celebration of love and presents. Growing up, even when we couldn't pay the rent, we always seemed to have lots of presents. The illusion was we were all okay – at Christmas anyway.

I loved the project, and was going to star with a well-known Australian actor named John Waters. Chris decided to join me for the Down Under experience. One of the locations we would be filming at was Ayers Rock, known for its healing qualities.

I was in the midst of fertility tests, and still trying to figure out why I couldn't conceive. My film liaison, who was assigned to take care of me, suggested that I do some tests in Sydney, considered Australia's leading fertility center. I decided to follow her advice.

We got there and started filming. I was fascinated with Australia. It reminded me of America in the 1950s: simpler, more open, more trustworthy. The people were available and loving and full of joy. The terrain was different and varied everywhere we went, from the rough Outback with its sparse spiritual essence to the beautiful, well-appointed and clean cities. There was an open-door policy for visits on the movie set, so I felt at home there too. Our winter was their summer, and we were just coming into it: warm days and brisk nights.

I had done some research and indeed New South Wales, which had a large kangaroo population, was also a hotspot for fertility expertise. So in the midst of working with these wonderful and talented people, who respected my creative process, I would go to a clinic in the early morning to be probed and prodded in my innermost sanctum. I wanted to keep this personal matter separate from the production, so we were always on a time restraint to get back. After reviewing all my other tests and my American doctors' inability to find the problem, they decided their best option was shooting dye through my Fallopian tubes to get a clear picture of any obstruction. It occurred to me that this was one of the first tests that should have been done years ago. Back to the zero point, as it were.

I was a little freaked out by the prospect, but the doctor assured me that it was no big deal – maybe I'd experience a slight discomfort that the tiny Valium pill would relieve. It didn't. What none of the other 'specialists' had found was a large fibroid tumor in one of my Fallopian tubes. When they shot the dye up me, it was like a massive, hurricane-force wave that hit a wall – the blockage in my tube. And I almost hit the roof. My screams sounded like something out of *The Exorcist*. The pain was so excruciating that I fainted on the table. When I awoke, I learned I had been recuperating for almost an hour.

'We have to go. You have to get back to the hotel. They're picking you up to drive out to the set in an hour,' my assistant said rather hurriedly. A very long pause ensued as I struggled to make sense of this in a slightly drugged state. 'Can you walk?' I guess I did; it was all a blur to me. Welcome to the actor's life.

We made it to the car with the aid of a wheelchair, and we arrived at the hotel, somehow got into the elevator, and started our climb to the room. She called Chris to meet us at the top. The door opened; I took one look at him and fainted dead away. I have always been lousy about pain. Chris freaked out a little and then this macho ex-marine swept me into his arms and carried me to the room. He put some ice in a towel and covered my face. While I was coming around, he was accosting my beautiful assistant – who had only been trying to help and did – with a myriad of questions and accusations about what had happened to his wife.

The poor woman was beside herself. There is nothing that gets me up and going faster than someone who needs rescuing, and so I sat up, albeit weakly, to defend her.

'Please,' she pleaded, 'I'll lose my job if they get wind of this. Please! I was only trying to help!'

I assured her this would stay between us. Besides, this test might have solved the riddle of my infertility, and I was grateful.

Chris looked at me. 'How the hell are you going to shoot? I'm not letting you go in this pain.'

I got up with all the fortitude and dignity my mother had shown so many times, and walked into the shower. Two hours later I was on the set, with Chris by my side. He wasn't about to let me out of his sight in case I had a relapse. For a marine, he sure was a teddy bear: a really strong, firm teddy bear. We started filming shortly afterward. It was a beautiful scene about a couple in old Australia and a flower that represented new beginnings and the birth of new energy. It was all my character had wanted for Christmas, but a drought had made it virtually impossible for anything to grow. The synchronicity with my own life didn't escape me, and sometimes when the message is so 'close to home,' it is more frightening to access.

We were working on a studio lot in town, but when you

stepped onto the set, you would have sworn you were in the Outback on that dusty and parched landscape around Ayers Rock. Even the dried garden resembled the barren land we would later visit. My character loved nature and the 'birth' of the winter flower. But there had been such a drought in the story that no blooms could be found. As the scene progresses, the character representing Santa materializes a beautiful, perfect flower stalk, and there is a heartfelt miracle moment between my husband and me. It was the kind of moment I'm known to capture. And I just couldn't get there. George came over to me and gently put his hand on my shoulder, looked into my eyes, and said, 'What is it, love?'

'I feel so much,' I told him. 'I feel so much that it won't come out.'

'Just give up then,' he smiled. 'Give up and don't do anything.'

I blinked. For an instant, I was back in class hearing Charles guide me to that blank page, to that zero point where nothing exists but the moment. I nodded my head. I heard 'Roll camera.' I heard 'Action,' and in that moment of nothingness a perfect scene was born.

The movie came out as a movie of the week on Disney in the States, and as a film in Australia. Well, I was sort of there. Half TV and half film was a good start. But the biggest gift, of course, was the news about the fibroid tumor. It was literally blocking my Fallopian tubes, so I couldn't receive the sperm. Again, I was a perfect creator. I can see now how the block that started in my energy system was now created materially in my body. Later I would learn that this is where all disease begins.

It was actually poetic. I had stopped nurturing my soul when my heart closed off. All that masculine energy directed at me had invoked my masculine side, and the female energy – that is, half of creation itself – had to be 'closed off.' I was, in essence, blocking my own nurturing. The sperm of life couldn't reach the egg of creation through the block. A metaphor of my life.

Again, I sought out help to rectify this situation. Nothing was going to keep me from creating this baby. But I was pushing the Universe so hard that all I was getting back was resistance. You can push against a cement wall until you're blue in the face, but the wall doesn't usually move. Most of us think that the more we push, the more we do, and the more we manipulate, the more we create the desired results. Not true. And I was learning that truism the hard way. And yet I still knew she was coming. I bought a Christmas ornament to put away until she arrived. I bought hand-knitted clothes for her hope chest. I dreamed about her. That baby girl was waiting for me, serving me, telling me to get over it and push on. And I was going to do it.

I found a wonderful doctor who confirmed the presence of the fibroid. But at that time, only major surgery was available to remove it, and I would be laid up for at least ten weeks, and then couldn't try to conceive for another six months to a year. I was thirty-eight and a half. This route wasn't a great option. My homeopathic physician suggested I see an acupuncturist named Daoshing Ni. He was a specialist in fertility. I went to him. I knew the first time we met that this was my best option. He would do this for me.

A visit with Dao started in a very clean, sparse room with a bed. He would take my pulse, look into my eyes, and ask me to stick out my tongue so he could calculate the temperature and the balance of my energy. I would always tease him and say, 'No, it's too personal,' and he would smile and say, 'Oh, please Dee, please,' and I would relent. He felt like my oriental big brother. I loved his soul immediately and trusted him implicitly. He promised me the needles were safe and clean, and the procedure wouldn't hurt. It didn't. I actually began asking for the one placed in the top of my head because it created such peace of mind. The other part of the remedy wasn't so easy. I spent the next few months drinking a ridiculously pungent tea to help expel whatever the hell the tumor was. Seriously, the first few times I tried it I threw up. The entire house would reek of this gross concoction. Chris used to say he was going to make the kid pay for enduring the smell. (He had yet to encounter poopy diapers.) Energetically, I suspected that anger and victimhood were showing up as the tumor in material form.

Dao also showed me how to run energy through my hands placed over the mass to help dissolve it. Little did I know that this was start-up training for the healing work I would be doing years later. I visited Dao twice a week for acupuncture treatments. He told me how energy worked, and gave me an unforgettable example of what happens when we block it. In China, when they passed the law that only one child per family would be allowed, the occurrence of fibroid tumors increased. Women were subconsciously making 'babies' the only way they could. I wondered why I had done the same instead of creating the real thing that I so desperately wanted. 'What caused this energetically?' I asked him one day.

'Babies are the height of the feminine creation,' Dao explained. 'The peak of a woman's creativity. Your feminine power has been blocked. When we dissolve the tumor, we will release that block so the new energy can flow. You can do your part by releasing it energetically.' What I had to release mostly was my anger. I had to get back to my magical self, and to that moment of nothingness where creation begins in an acting scene or when moving through your life. The experience on E.T. kept defining my self-creation, and like a bad acting experience, I kept trying to create my life from an old idea. I wasn't allowing myself to be open to all the possibilities that NO IDEA brings forth. In my perspective, I had been thwarted by so much male energy that I had shut down my feminine side to survive. Dee needed to 'get back home.' Dee needed to love and nurture herself again. I needed a brand-new day of nothing where everything is possible. And so, as my Australian director had suggested, I gave up. I gave up trying to get pregnant. Six years of trying was enough. I gave up pushing. And I gave up testing. I surrendered.

During this time, I kept doing projects, some good and some bad. I had the enormous pleasure of working with Tommy Lee Jones on a movie of the week called *Stranger on My Land*. Another gruff teddy bear, Tommy took me into his heart once he saw I wasn't some wussie little broad that couldn't ride a horse. I did all my own riding, which made me one of the boys. He and his wife were trying to have a baby. I passed Dao's information along to them. It was important to share it with them. I find this is usually true: the Universe draws you into a project for more important reasons than doing an acting gig, or getting involved in a relationship, or taking a new job – it's a constant mirror effect for all of us. And the project itself was, again, about someone threatening my family and my home, but this time they weren't furry little hairballs. This time it was the government, the biggest representation of suits and power ball in the material world. Keep the lessons coming, Universe! I'm starting to wake up! And my life was about to change forever.

Chris and I had been at a celebrity baseball game when it happened. We did a lot of celebrity charity events, and on this particular day we had been playing baseball to raise money for an animal shelter. Chris had originally wanted to be a baseball player and had actually come out from New Hampshire to audition for the Los Angeles Dodgers. While waiting for tryouts, he paid his way working as a tour guide at one of the major studios. An executive spotted him, put him under contract, and the rest, as they say, is history. On this day, after he had smacked one out of the park, I was up next. I wasn't great at this but I tried. 'Just keep your eye on the ball, Pupper!' he would yell. 'Treat it like your partner, and try to connect!' And I hit it and made it to second base. Everybody cheered. But my home run came when we walked back into our home and I checked the message machine. There was a message from my chiropractor. I hadn't told Chris about my late period after so many false alarms and energy depletions around me getting pregnant. I did tell my chiropractor, who had been on this ride with me now for six years, about being late. 'I'll order a test,' he offered. 'Nobody else has to know.'

I pushed the message button with my heart in my throat.

'Dee,' I heard his voice echo. Was it a good tone? A sad tone? A doctor tone? 'Dee, it's Joe; if you're there, pick up.' A small pause. 'Damn it. Congratulations, Dee! You're pregnant.'

Time stopped. I looked at Chris. The kitchen floor turned into a field of yellow daffodils as I tried to make my way in what felt like slow motion into his arms. When I got there, he swept me up and twirled me like a prom queen. I searched his eyes. 'Tell me you're happy, baby,' I said with tears now flowing out of my very happy blue eyes. 'Tell me you're happy.'

He looked overwhelmed. His eyes filled with tears. 'I'm happy, Pupper, I'm happy. And I'm scared to death.' I had never seen him cry, and I had never seen him scared. The energetic responsibility had catapulted him into total vulnerability. I don't think I ever loved him more than in that moment.

In giving up, I had allowed myself to go to the zero point. Hell, there was nowhere else to go. If we just knew that we could – and must – create from that place, maybe we wouldn't have to create so many scenarios that force us there: my six years of fertility testing, or for others a financial lack, life-threatening illness, or abusive relationships. Maybe we could simply go to that place of nothingness that allows everything and plays out the scenes of our lives brilliantly the first time. We would have a lot more home runs.

The next week my obstetrician confirmed the test again. I was indeed pregnant. I was given orders to not work for nine months: the strain of the emotional work I was always hired for and the exhaustion that usually came with filming wasn't okay. This was a high-risk pregnancy because of my age. It is the only time in my life I can remember when I gave myself permission not to work and simply trust enough to give up. And it was amazing.

'You'll kill somebody,' my best friend said.

'You not work? Not be busy? You'll go bonkers,' my brother chided.

But I didn't. It was easy. It was easy to do it for her. I would do anything for her. She was already teaching me how to love myself through this miracle that I had created. And I knew. I knew it was all going to be perfect. And it was. My backaches went away, I never had a day of morning sickness, and I was never as happy in my life. And despite his fears, so was Chris.

We would go to dinner with friends and he would tell his favorite story from Lamaze class. All the expectant fathers were in a circle, sharing the progress of the pregnancy and helping each other deal with the preparations, both emotional and physical. This particular day they were discussing the baby's room and sharing each other's progress. Chris was at the end of the circle. As each person had his turn, some would share that they hadn't really gotten started yet, while some were painting the nursery, and others were selecting wallpaper. Some of the guys had gone shopping with their wives to choose furniture, and a few were waiting to find out the sex of their child before they did anything. They got to Chris.

'It's all done,' he stated flatly.

'What do you mean?' the leader asked.

'It's done. We painted the room, bought the furniture, purchased the clothes, washed and hung them up, and even put the diapers under the changing table. It's done.'

'Wow,' one of the guys responded. 'But, but … what if something happens, or it's a different sex than you expected?'

According to Chris, he gave this guy his best 'back-off, buddy' marine stare, took in the entire circle, and replied, 'She knows. She's always known. Everything's going to be perfect.'

Nine months later – well, nine months, two weeks, twenty-four hours of labor, and some harrowing last few moments later

– I was holding my beautiful daughter in my arms. And yes, she was perfect. Every little toe, finger, and dimple was absolutely perfect. Of course, she could have looked like Yoda and I would have felt the same way.

Chris often called her Conehead, after the *Saturday Night Live* skits. The umbilical cord had become wrapped around her neck, and so they had to suction her and use forceps, and all that contributed to a very pointed little head upon arrival. He actually started smoking again in the labor room. I really didn't know what was going on, but I guess the cord around her neck made her heart rate drop, and my blood pressure soared. I heard my doctor say something to the effect of 'If we don't get her out in the next push, we'll have to do a C Section.' Screw that! I thought. I didn't go through twenty-four hours of labor for nothing. Every dancer muscle in my body united in the biggest push of the century, and out popped Gabrielle. Gabrielle Elise Bourassa. My Little Girl. I had torn a picture of a baby out of a book some months earlier and shown it to Chris. 'She's going to look like this.'

He had smiled. 'Sure, Pupper,' he answered, placating me. And she did.

And with the birth of my daughter, I was reborn. My heart was open, because I wanted to teach her and have her experience only love in her life. So I had to be that example for her. I was her teacher, and I always learned the most when I taught others.

And I had taught many. I had already taught Sunday school, had my own dance studio, and taught high school. I had touched many lives already, and had made a difference in my own because I had made a difference in theirs. I recall an unhappy, underprivileged student who warned me not to get into my car after school one day. It would blow up. He was pretending to have rigged it – to get attention, I assumed.

I looked him straight in the eyes. 'I love you, Alan,' I said. 'I love you enough not to believe you. I'll be getting in my car because I trust you.' At three o'clock, I walked to my car, got in, and drove away.

The next morning he was there when I arrived. With tears in his eyes, he walked up, took a deep breath, and proclaimed, 'I'm sorry, Ms Wallace. I think you're the bravest person I've ever met.' And then he collapsed into my arms. Alan became an A student and one of my closest student friends.

And then there was my Basic English class: the outcasts for whom no one held any high expectations. 'Don't take them past a paragraph. Half of them can't write their name,' my supervisor smirked. But by the end of the year, they were writing three-page themes. Because I believed they could do so much, they believed it. The themes were about motorcycles and hot rods and tattoos. But theme papers they were, nevertheless.

And now I wanted to teach my little girl. I wanted to be the best mom there ever was. I wanted to be MY mom. If I can be as true and loving as my mother, I will serve her well, I thought. I was determined not to teach her fear, or lack, or smallness, only about the best in herself and others. And I would find the best in me again for her. I would find my zero point and teach from there.

Four months later, while I was still breastfeeding, Al Burton called again. They had found a direct descendant of Lassie, and he was going to do a series called *The New Lassie*. A direct descendant. I remember thinking how I grew up watching Lassie. At the end of every show, I would be crying uncontrollably, and turn to my beloved Skipper and exclaim, 'You could do that, girl. You'd save me. I just know you would!' And here I was, back at the beginning, and with 'a direct descendant.' Interesting.

'So,' Al poked, 'are you interested? And by the way, we would love to have Chris play the husband.'

I am sure that over the years, outsiders thought I demanded to work with Chris or I wouldn't do the project. That simply wasn't the case. Producers just offered him the supporting parts. Maybe it was because our very clear intention when we married was that we wouldn't be apart for long periods. Or was it the built-in chemistry between us that lit up the screen or tube? All I know is that I asked to be together, and the Universe delivered.

So the offer was out, but I had a lot of concerns about Gaby. I didn't want my child to be raised by a nanny. I had one, but it was clear in her job description that I was hands-on, and her obligations included shopping, etc., so I could spend time with my baby.

'Because of the budget,' Al ventured, 'we can't go overtime. I won't bring you in till nine, or work you past six, and I'll give you a two-hour lunch break to be with her. What do you say?' What do you think? My heart leapt. I had hit that zero point where I gave up, and creation was happening again. Either way, I had always been a perfect creator, like all of us. But I was so much happier creating what I wanted, instead of replaying the traumas of yesteryear.

The Universe offered me a steak dinner with all the trimmings. I received the order and feasted happily for two seasons. I had three hours with Gaby in the morning, put her to bed every night, and had one-on-one time with her for two hours in the middle of every day. We would take our little golf cart and go tootling around Universal Studios, visiting Fievel's Playground, seeing the fake flood, and visiting Jaws. I am proud to say she was never frightened about the scary shark. In fact, her first complete sentence was, 'Mommy. See big fish.' Very Hollywood. Is it any wonder she grew up to be an actress?

Chris stepped up and directed four episodes that were tremendously successful. We were a complete family, on and off the screen. I felt my joy again. I felt my light again. And I desperately wanted to share that with the world. Chris had supported me through all of this travail: financially, psychologically, physically, and spiritually, and he never balked at giving me the spotlight. He loved his daughter without limits, and I'm happy he was so celebrated in his directorial efforts. This was as good as it got. I didn't realize at the time how true that was going to be.

Chapter Ten

Surrender

The New Lassie ended and the dog days of summer returned: parched, slow, and lazy. Work had essentially dried up. I had returned to the Zero Point, but wasn't creating anything from it. Yes, television sprinkled its infrequent offerings my way, but there weren't enough to make the mortgage payment. Chris was working sporadically, too. Somebody had to do something. And true to form, when someone needs help, here I come. And so I stepped forward to do the next best thing I knew: teach. Little did I know that, like the famous movie, the Universe was yelling, 'Surrender, Dorothy!' I had to get back home as surely as E.T. did. I just couldn't find the way.

In recent years, Charles had gradually brought in advanced students to teach some classes for him. He wanted more time off and understandably so. Teaching five classes a week is exhausting, no matter how much you love the process. By the time I finished *Lassie,* Charles was retiring from teaching. This was a huge heart hit for me. Even if I hadn't been to class for a while, I knew it was always there, my port in the storm. Like the lover you think you'll always hook up with again and then he gets married, Charles' retirement left a big hole in my life. Camelot was gone. I would have to find a new acting home.

In retrospect I think this was divine timing. I would have never started a studio if his was still up and running. I had too much esteem for my mentor and too much honor to even think I might replace him in any way. But the Conrad Studio was defunct, and Charles was moving to North Carolina. And I needed to make a living. And so I decided to create an acting studio of my own. Gaby's birth had also opened a place of sharing within me. I wanted to give from my heart again, and teaching had always brought me great joy by positively affecting others. It was, I thought, also a way to honor the man who had changed my life: I wanted to bring his teachings forward in an honest, authentic way so a new generation of actors could experience these life-changing shifts.

It did occur to me that I might be compromising myself. I was an actress. Wouldn't this be pulling my focus away from my art? As if perfectly orchestrated, I happened upon a special about Steve Allen that highlighted his many talents: author, satirist, actor, host, and composer. When asked how he juggled them all, he simply replied, 'I'm passionate about them all. I wake up and feel which passion I want to create with that day.' It was a truth that resonated with me. I chose in that moment to surrender to another passion in my life: teaching people how to live in their hearts through acting.

All the pieces of this puzzle came together. As I would learn in the future, pure intention often creates the work of art for you. The Universe simply takes you on a ride if you let it. One of my best friends, an actress that I hugely admired from the Studio, had gone off to New York and started the very successful Sally Johnson Studio. Charles' instinctive approach was valued in a city where stage acting was trying to learn film technique. Whenever I visited New York, I would watch her teach, and marvel at her rapport with students and what she had created there. When my life reached this stage, Sally came forward to suggest that I open an LA studio. She even offered to make me copies of her scenes and exercises to give me a jump-start. It was a big help. The right material is the secret for pushing actors through a block and guiding them into a joyful awareness of themselves. Like life, the material helps form the intention. I was learning to look for the open doors, and to say yes.

At the same time, a young actor from a musical I had produced was the liaison to a casting director. This CD had decided to open a showcase venue that would offer actors many different teachers and workshops, a one-stop place where an actor could find everything and drop a lot of money. My friend called to see if I would be interested in teaching a class. Synchronicity? They would do the advertising and refer people etc., which appealed to me: once again, it was easier for me to split the business and the creative. In my naiveté I thought I would have at least one full class straightaway. I mean, I was a pretty big name with a lot of credits. I was a working actor. People could see that I knew my craft. That didn't seem to make much difference. In my first class, I had five students.

But the Universe had set this up rather easily, and I was along for the ride. I decided to stick it out. Truth is, I loved teaching this approach so much that it was a no-brainer, whatever the return. I had dug out all of Charles' old handouts and reviewed them. Thank God I had saved everything, just like my mother did. This was valuable reference material now, and so much of the basic actor's training came back to me again. But what should I do first? It reminded me of that song from *The Sound of Music*: 'Let's start at the very beginning. A very good place to start.' That good old blank page – it makes you go back to your instinct every time. So I decided to begin by going down this road exactly as I had done, so many years earlier.

Like my mentor, I began the first hour teaching about energy and how it worked. I wanted to be brilliant, so of course I did everything I knew NOT to do: I over-planned down to the last detail. I had notes written out down to the proverbial exclamation mark. I had retrieved reams of handouts from my Charles file to share with my students. I got about five minutes into the 'lesson,' and one of the girls interrupted me.

'What does this have to do with acting?' she challenged. I explained that actors work with energy, and that high energy gets us out of our heads and into our instincts, and therefore understanding energy seemed like a good place to start. 'Great,' she quipped. 'Can't we just act?'

I have to admit that I got a little pissed off. I could feel my control taking a nosedive into the toilet. This student was forcing me to live in the moment, the very core of the method itself. I told her to get up. She did. I told her to see a monster, to react, scream, and run across the room; get attacked and die as she rolled down the wall. She looked at me and blinked. She started laughing. I yelled, 'NOW!' She did a somewhat lame B-movie rendition of a pathetic death scene – one she probably saw in a movie. I'm sure the class of five students wondered if they had walked into their own horror film. I quickly turned around and executed a brilliant monster-attacking-the-blonde-in-the-backyard scene.

One of the other students got up. 'I want to try,' she said excitedly. She gave it a go and was pretty good. Then the next three followed, and afterward we talked about how high energy releases us from our mental maps and allows us to create from our own intuitive channel. Finally, the first girl asked if she could do the scene again. She did and it was much better.

I threw out the note structure of playing it safe and ran with being in the moment. I had a plethora of new information of my own to add to this amazing technique. While working with doctors on getting pregnant, I had learned Kinesiology, and also how to direct and focus energy. It was amazing to me just how much new information I had gathered and could apply to acting. Trying to understand the underlying beliefs that kept creating negative perceptions and patterns had been made dramatically easier with Kinesiology, or muscle testing. It was a way to test the truthfulness of a true subconscious belief versus what the conscious mind thought. Later we talked briefly about the life fears we were running away from, and how these kept us from walking into our work.

'Oh my God,' the girl said quietly. 'That's how I feel when I go to get an agent. I'm afraid they'll abandon me like my mom did.'

I didn't use the muscle testing for a while. But I knew I would eventually. It was these types of revelations that begged for it. Kinesiology had opened up for me a whole new understanding of the subconscious that I could share with students. I wasn't showing them how to do it technically yet, just teaching them the principles, as I kept diligently working with various alternative doctors who were exploring this technique.

This certainly was one of my unique additions to Charles' already solid instinctive technique. I was hungry to share with the students about love and acceptance. No one had learned these lessons better than I. And I was determined, as I had been at the birth of my daughter, to teach them to release anger and live in harmony. That wasn't possible if you were as pissed off about the business end of 'show biz' as Charles and I had been for many years. You simply had to love the energy around what you wanted to be a part of. They needed to surrender their egos, let go, and create from a new perspective. And in teaching that, I was relearning it at deeper levels myself.

I knew I was a good communicator from other teaching venues, but I feel my love of acting and my expertise combined to make me an awesome acting teacher. In one of my first classes, I had a beautiful female student (she ended up staying for six years) who simply couldn't get through an emotional block. She was real, she was in the moment, but she just couldn't get 'there.'

'Why can't I do this?' she demanded. 'Every class I go to, it's the same thing. Can YOU tell me?' Wow. What a way to put a new teacher on the spot.

'Take a breath and give up. Stop trying. Nobody gives a damn whether you break down.'

'But it SAYS, *and she breaks down*. And I can't just forget the directions,' she countered.

I instructed her. 'Just try what I'm suggesting. Just give up.'

'But then I won't get the damn job,' she countered.

How do you move someone to surrender and try something new when the person believes that surrendering is not safe? How could I teach the lesson that the other female student had drawn out of me that first day? Now I knew how Charles had felt at times. In their minds we become gods that are supposed to have all the answers and save them. Even when they don't choose it. And in an instant flash it came to me.

'Get up,' I commanded.

'Why?'

'GET UP.' It was the best Charles-voice I could muster. It must have been close: she stood up. 'Okay,' I told her. 'I'm the person who has hurt you the most in your life. I'm going to hold up my hands, and I want you to keep pushing them and yelling "GET AWAY!" until I tell you to pick up your scene. Then go straight to that part.'

We proceeded to do the exercise. 'GET AWAY, GET AWAY, GET AWAY!' she kept screaming.

'Pick up the scene!' I yelled. She did and began her lines. The moment came. The tears flowed. The scene ended. The room was silent, and then it exploded with applause. The door opened and the manager demanded, 'What the hell is going on in here?'

'I just broke through the biggest damn block in my acting!' the girl yelled back, still reeling in emotional angst.

'Oh,' he said, and backed out and closed the door. It was a moment.

That was my technique. This was mined from hours of emotional work on a live set. I knew that it often takes a physical expression of energy to break through to an emotional one. I flew home to tell Chris and share.

He looked at me calmly. 'Pupper, you're so cute. You're the only one who is ever surprised at how great you are.' Later Chris would patiently sit and listen after each class about the breakthroughs and the new students and new exercises that were helping them discover themselves.

From years on working sets, I had practical know-how and lots of techniques unavailable to Charles. For instance, when you're doing a very dramatic role, you often have to act at many different locations and at different times – like weeks apart! It can be confusing and emotionally exhausting. I would show the students how to play the core part of the scene full out, but use eye drops in their eyes to stimulate tears while running to the car that usually was shot two weeks later. You simply didn't have to get the same emotional charge for the car scene. It was okay to 'act' with a little help. And then later, when you get to the interior of the car and have another emotional dialogue scene, you move back into the technique. I even taught a class on how to hit marks, and do over-the-shoulder shots and close-ups, so they knew what to expect on a set. And I loved it. And I loved them. And they knew it. They knew that all the pushing and prodding, yelling and cajoling, were because I loved them unconditionally. Together we could do just about anything. It was empowering. It was joyful. And it was healing.

By teaching my students, I was re-teaching myself. I knew all too well their fears, their stories, how they had been damaged by well-meaning people, and how they had limited themselves. I had experienced it all. And as the days went by, I realized that the studio was as much about healing as acting. People were being healed and becoming happier and more balanced. And I was, too. It was so apparent that many of these talented people had fallen prey to the erroneous beliefs that the more you suffered, paid your dues, and were dirt poor, the more it made you a better actor. It gave you more 'fuel' to stoke the creative fire. I wanted them to know they could live happy, balanced lives, and choose to be a screwed-up character when the cameras rolled. I was teaching this from instinct, from a place I knew.

It became increasingly apparent that the beliefs they held were also limiting their lives out in the world – as it did their acting careers. Bottom line: as you believe, it will be delivered unto you. In one class, we discovered that every time a particular student entered a new relationship, all of her auditioning and work would come to a halt. She had watched her mom become successful after a volatile divorce from her dad, and that experience equaled this belief in her life: happy relationships and success don't go together. We marveled more and more about how the acting technique was simply a metaphor for our own lives. I didn't know why this was becoming such an integral part of the class. Only that it was important.

I had soon increased to two almost-full classes, had begun doing scene nights to show off my students to agents, etc., when the Universe stepped in again with the perfect taxi ride to the next stop. One of my most soulful students was the daughter of a female minister at a Science of Mind church called Spiritworks. She had shared the work we were doing in acting class with her mother, who was enthralled. When I began looking for my own place, Christina approached me with an offer.

'I told my mom about you, and she wants your energy in the church. There's a great downstairs space, and it's free. And she doesn't care if you attend. No strings attached.' Incredible things click when you are joyously creating your life, and you give up and allow.

I went to look at it. It was perfect: small enough to be intimate and big enough to expand into the workshop venues that I was planning. I never hesitated. I got in the taxi. Somehow, I could get out of the way again when it came to teaching and receiving and trusting the Universe to take me along for the ride. I moved all the studio stuff to the church, set up shop, and never looked back. I taught there for the next six months, when the call came.

I had an audition the next day for a film. A big studio film. The first one in years. It was for Peter Jackson, who had just directed *Heavenly Creatures*, which was one of the most amazing films I had ever seen. I was beside myself with excitement and fear. I had remembered from teaching this to my students: you can't want it too much, because behind that need is the fear you won't get it. You have to go into an audition with the simple intention of loving to do the material, loving to do the part, being in the moment. I kept taking deep breaths all the way to Universal Studios.

I walked into a small, dark little impromptu theater and there was Peter Jackson. Another big teddy bear. He introduced himself. He was wearing shorts and flip-flops, had a big bushy beard, and slightly resembled one of the hobbits that would soon make him famous. We discussed the part. I got up. Just as I was about to launch, Michael J. Fox entered. 'Hey, sorry I'm late.' Peter started to introduce us and Michael interrupted him. 'I know Dee. Hey, Dee. We met ...'

'Last year,' I answered. 'How are you, Michael?'

'Good. Really good. I'm so glad you could come in for this.' There was something really genuine about his tone. I always loved Michael. He was a little shy and soft-spoken and genuine.

'Look. Please try to see me with black hair,' I said, pointing to my bleached blonde head. 'I just don't see her like this.'

'Good point, love,' Peter responded. I began. I knew this character: the woman was the perceived victim of a maniac but was actually the strong person who had helped murder everyone. This was another metaphor about my life: by seeing myself as a victim, I had murdered my creative self. I flipped out before their very eyes, and ended in a dead faint as scripted. I held it a moment for dramatic effect as I had taught my students to do, and got up. 'Brilliant, Dee. Brilliant. Thanks so much for coming in.'

Michael gave me a hug, and I was on my way home. The next day they booked me. Six weeks later I would be on my way to New Zealand for the shoot. It didn't escape me that I had found the light again. And I had it back because I had opened my heart and was giving again through my acting class. And because I was giving again, I received something in return. This was my first studio film in fifteen years.

An interesting thing happened to me at this point. Part of me didn't want to leave. I just didn't want to leave my students. And I had worked so hard to make the studio successful. 'How odd,' I told Chris. 'Money was the intention for creating this venue, and now it has been replaced with its own purpose and with love. Nice.'

'Just as long as you know you'll have to start over when you get back,' Chris added. 'But you gotta do this. It's what you've wanted to create for yourself.'

This may have been his fear of 'having to start over,' but it was also mine as well. When people show up and express fears and limitations to you, they are simply mirroring what you are holding. They are coming forward so you can receive it and shift yourself into knowingness. Unfortunately, most of us accept our fears as a realistic prediction of what's happening to us. If we accept the suggestion, we risk the chance of forming a belief that limits us. And as we all know, 'As you believe, it is delivered unto you.'

I looked my lover in the eye. He had been my first teacher of New Age principles. Now I could return the favor. 'I'm choosing to believe that I will have a studio when I get back. They'll all be here. It will be easy.'

There was a long silence between us. Chris swept me up into his arms. 'Thanks,' the marine said softly, 'for reminding me.' I often wondered during these times how Chris was feeling. He was a proud man and work had dried up considerably for him. It seemed that he had lost some of his life force, which happens to us when we allow our definition of success or its lack to run our lives. It must have been difficult not knowing how to provide for us, and watching me move from the acting that I loved to teaching to help us to survive. We had had discussions about what else he thought he might be able to do, and he would smile and wonder if there was a geriatric baseball team needing a centerfielder. Deep in my heart, I pushed the ache away. We would be okay. We were here forever together.

I said aloha to my students with all their email addresses written down to keep them updated. Gaby would accompany me to New Zealand with our nanny for a visit, and then return to Chris, who would stay in LA so afterward she could remain in school. He was working at the time doing a small role and couldn't come anyway. I wanted him to feel good about himself. Seventeen years together had created a safety net of trust.

So off I went with daughter, nanny, and best wishes from my students. We arrived after a very long flight and were greeted by my beautiful handler, and taken to a gorgeous apartment that I would call home for the next six weeks. We had a day to recoup. And then started the process of wig fittings and costume adjustments. Fran, Peter's partner, personally and professionally, oversaw everything. We were all discussing Patricia's 'look' and how it was going to change throughout the picture. She had to go from a weak, victimized, dowdy woman to being taken over by the primal force of her perverse younger self. They showed me sketches of some their ideas.

'Personally,' I offered, 'I think she should look younger as she goes along.'

'But she's older,' Fran said.

'But her energy gets younger as she reclaims the charge and excitement she had when they were on their killing spree. She comes alive all over again.'

Fran smiled. 'Dee, that's brilliant. That's exactly what we're going to do.' Yes, I would enjoy this detour the Universe had brought me.

For the next week our nanny Kristen, Gaby, and I toured around Wellington, New Zealand and saw the local sights. Then I got a call from the production manager. There was going to be a delay. Peter wanted some rewrites. We wouldn't be filming for another three weeks, and they would like to send us all on a trip around New Zealand for a little holiday while we were waiting. Cool. So the three of us had an unforgettable trip around one of the most beautiful countries in the world, and the home to some of the warmest, nicest people I have ever met. We created some memorable experiences that have lasted a lifetime.

When we returned, I was to start shooting in two days. Gaby and Kristen packed up to head home, and although I loved having my daughter there, school beckoned and Chris was missing her. The next afternoon I got a call that there were more rewrites, and when I got the revised script, everything about my character had changed. This especially applied to her intentions. And I had my biggest scene the next morning at 6:00 A.M. Again, prayers of thanks went out to my mentor for teaching a technique that allowed me to create in the moment.

Shooting started and was going great. I was having a ball playing Patricia. Finally, I got to show the sadistic side of Dee Wallace and it was more fun than I can tell you. In fact, it was cathartic: I was able to release enormous amounts of buried anger and grief that I had accumulated over years from the numerous tragedies of life. I was pleased that, by this time, I knew how to return to 'me' after Patricia had lived in me during twelve-hour days. Some actors can't. It's not healthy. But, on the set, I continued finding these outrageous dark parts of myself that to my surprise were extremely easy to access.

I had gotten up to make my morning tea. It was four hours later next day in Los Angeles. The telephone rang. It was Kristen. Her voice sounded bad. A mother can read the timbre of her nanny's breath.

'What?' I demanded. Hesitation. 'WHAT? Is she all right?' Another pause. 'TALK TO ME!'

'Gaby's fine, Dee. She's fine. But Chris has had a heart attack.' The next few moments were experienced like energetic mud. My vision went blurry. My heart went into palpitations. 'He's okay. He's stabilized. We were playing baseball at the park. But it was pretty bad. They have to do surgery.'

I told Kristen, 'Don't you leave Gaby's side. Keep her routine as normal as possible. But don't lie to her about anything. And Kristen, make sure she knows this was not her fault. I'll be there. I'll call you back.' I spoke to my little girl and told her Mommy was on the way. I hung up and called Josie, my handler, who had become my confidante and friend. 'My husband has had a heart attack. I need you.' She could hear the tears flowing.

Within thirty minutes came two producers, Josie, and three other members of the crew with whom I was close. Within two hours I was scheduled on a flight home. When I talked to Peter, concerned about the shoot, he simply replied, 'It's just a movie, Dee. This is your life. Go home and take care of your family.' What a guy, and a great director.

I boarded the plane for the twenty-hour flight back to the States. Everything was done for me and I was appreciative, to say the least. When I finally arrived, I called Kristen. Chris had had more heart attacks at the hospital. She was there. 'Can I talk to him?'

The nurse put him on. 'Hey, Pupper,' he said weakly.

'I'm coming, Toff. I'll be there soon.'

When I got to the hospital, Chris wouldn't let me see him till he was cleaned up. He had been barfing up his guts and thought he looked bad. Always the marine.

I tried to walk in with my bravest face on, but when I saw him I broke down crying. He looked so fragile and weak – and helpless. He smiled. 'Just needed some attention, did we?' I joked.

'Yeah,' he countered, 'and some hot sex.' We managed a laugh. But our eyes could not disguise all the fear and pain we were feeling.

They did the angioplasty. It went okay. When the doctor came in to check on him, he found us both curled up in each other's arms asleep in the hospital bed. Jet lag and surgery can sure knock a couple out. He informed us that all was well, that Chris was lucky. He'd have to stay for two days, and then he could go home to recuperate. Chris was never a good patient, but he agreed.

I went to take care of my other patient: a very scared little girl who needed to be in her mommy's arms. I called the doctor and asked him if he would talk to her and assure her that it wasn't her fault. It wasn't hospital protocol at all, but I had helped heal enough students to know that incorrect perceptions of childhood events can affect you for the rest of your life. I wanted to do what I could to set the record straight in the mind of this little seven-year-old. She seemed to accept his authority and became somewhat more peaceful about it. We played house and Candy Land, and she asked if she could have a sleepover. Good, I thought. She knows how to soothe herself.

The next day I spent at the hospital. Kristen brought Gaby down to visit. Chris was up and feeling pretty darn good. This was one exciting ride that I could have lived without, but we all made it through and Chris seemed fine. My agent called to inquire about my availability: the studio wanted to know if I was coming back, or should they reshoot or make other arrangements. I was torn. Chris was clear. Go.

We called the doctor in for a consultation. 'Your husband's out of the woods,' he said. 'And as long as he takes it easy for a month, he'll be good as new.'

Chris looked at me and said firmly, 'Go.'

I couldn't ask the studio to fly Gaby and Kristen back again, and I couldn't afford to pay their way. I left with the agreement that Kristen would stay night and day for at least a week and then we would go from there.

So five days after traveling halfway around the world, I was back on a twenty-hour flight to New Zealand. I had no idea how all this stress was affecting me physically and psychologically. I was just always taught to be a trooper and keep going. So I did.

I arrived back, had half a day, and went straight to the set. They had been juggling the shooting schedule for me, holding up some of my scenes until I returned. The next three days were great. I spoke to Chris and Gaby three or four times a day. On Wednesday night I called. 'Gaby lost a tooth, Pupper. How much should the little fairy leave?' Chris asked.

'Let's leave her a dollar. The kid's earned it,' I joked.

'I'm doing great,' he offered so I wouldn't have to ask. 'Go do your job. Everything is fine. I'll take care of her tooth.' We said we loved each other. It was the last time I would hear him say that.

The next morning the phone rang. It was Kristen. 'What NOW?' I asked, with my stress load at capacity. Silence. 'What?' I demanded. Silence. 'WHAT!!!'

'Chris is dead. He had another heart attack. He didn't make it.'

I remember my body went into total shock. Like an internal earthquake, I felt the shockwaves roll through me. My knees gave out. 'Oh my God. Oh my God. Oh my God.' That's all I could say over and over again. And then I came back. 'Where is Gaby?'

'She's fine. She's here with me. But Dee, she found him.'

A primal scream erupted from my soul. NO! I thought. She was supposed to have a perfect life! She wasn't supposed to lose her dad, too. 'Put her on the phone,' I demanded. 'Gab. I know you're scared. I know you're sad. Mommy is coming home as fast as she can.'

Her little voice quivered. 'Mommy, can you hurry?'

I couldn't. The next flight out wasn't until the following day. I hung up. I called Josie. I told her what had happened. An instant replay of the earlier rescue mission went into action: within minutes everyone was there, including a doctor this time. He gave me a mild sedative. I called the mother of Gaby's best friend. Could she take Gaby for the day? Have a play date? 'Of course,' she said. I called our business manager of twenty years.

'Don't think about anything. I'm on the way to the house. I'll make all the arrangements.'

'Cremation,' I answered. 'That's what he wanted. And a party. No service.'

We had talked about these arrangements almost jokingly. Chris had told me when we got married that he was going to go first, and that he wanted me to move on and be happy. He believed that he was going to pass on at the age of fifty-five, but he always kidded about it. I guess I didn't want to face it either. So we both denied what he seemed to know as a certainty. As I said earlier, he had a brain aneurism some years before we met, and had actually gone through the tunnel of light. To see the peacefulness on the face of this masculine god as he told this story was remarkable. I often think now that he just couldn't wait to experience that again. Chris was fifty-four when he passed on.

I told my manager that I wanted sixties music played at the party. Chris would have been happy without anything. Never gonna happen, I would say. 'Okay, babe. But have everybody say what a great guy I was.'

And at his celebration, everyone did. It wasn't hard. He was loved and cherished by so many people in and out of the business. Gaby had come to me with her own ideas. She wanted to release balloons so Daddy would be happy up in the sky, and some of those white birds that made everything peaceful. Doves. A beautiful thought. A good friend collected some of our pictures and put together a beautiful video tribute that we played at the party. I set out a table for all his achievements, including his newly finished children's book on Creation. My family all came to support me.

And within a week, I was back on a plane with Gaby and Kristen to finish filming. I truly don't know how I did it. But I did let go. I surrendered. The Universe carried me. I wasn't able to carry myself. At one point, I was doing a scene where I have to shoot Michael's character. It was surreal: when I shot him, it was Michael. When he hit the ground, it was Chris. And then I am pulled into the tunnel of light. Like some four-year-old, I was unable to distinguish between the fantasy and reality of life. I had hit that zero point again. We finished shooting, and I flew home and walked into the house with all the memories we had managed to escape from while in New Zealand. Where was my life at now? Where could I go with what I had? Did I have the energy to start anew on my own? I looked at my beautiful daughter: my purpose, my joy, my heart. I would find me. For her, I could do anything. But after my father's suicide, the loss of my career, and now my dear husband's death, I was on my knees. Literally. I gave up, cried out, and asked for a way that people could heal themselves. And what happened next was beyond my wildest comprehension.

Chapter Eleven

Just Know

Walking back into that house was like walking into purgatory as I understood it. Limbo. The stagnation of not being able to move anywhere. Stuck between heaven and hell. It had occurred to me that in *The Frighteners* my character, who appeared to be the quintessential victim, was actually the mass murderer: I was still the victim but of my own weapons of self-hatred, fear, and judgment.

I moved in slow motion through the sea of memories and the vibrations of my life with Chris there. I was ready for a new script: *A Woman Understands the Meaning of Her Life.* But who would write my screenplay? One night, after I put Gaby to bed, the panic started to rise up in my chest. I was alone, without support, in a cold, dark, scary house and this represented my world as I envisioned it. I panicked. I was breaking down. I fell to my knees and yelled out, 'I don't want to do this anymore! I need a break here, God! I want to be happy! I want to be happy, damn it! And I want a way we can all heal ourselves. Now.' Reams of tears poured down my face. I convulsed. I coughed. I ended up lying in a fetal position on the floor in the dining room. Then I heard a voice in my head. 'Use the light within you to heal E.T.' What? 'Use the light within you to heal E.T.'

That was how it started. That was the first time I heard 'the voice.' I silently asked myself, How do I do that? At least I wasn't talking out loud to the dog yet. 'Just know,' was the reply. Know? 'Just Know.' I lay there on the floor for some time. I was feeling kind of peaceful. It was like after you found out that there is no Santa Claus, railed against the injustice, and then realized that Santa had been lots of people loving you for a long time. 'Okay.

I know I want to heal myself and be happy, and want a way that people can heal themselves. And I choose to know that it will come.' I fell asleep on the floor with that Knowing. Three hours later I woke up and put myself to bed. I slept for ten hours.

The next thing I heard was Gaby's baby voice coming over the monitor: 'Mamamamamama.' I used to love that in the morning, that human alarm clock of love calling for me. My German Shepherd came over for her morning pat on the head. 'Hey girl,' I said. 'Sounds like Gab is ready to play.' And then I sat straight up in bed. Gaby was seven now. What the hell was I hearing? I was conscious. I hadn't been dreaming. I was back to the past. I was here, but I was also there. Knowing had reminded me of when I had experienced that true state earlier. I ran to her room. She was asleep in the midst of all her stuffies, much like the closet scene from *E.T.* Looking at her, my heart swelled. At that moment I had a glimpse in my love for her of what it was to 'know.'

I called my assistant. 'Can you come in today?' I asked. She wasn't supposed to start for another week, but didn't even ask why. She arrived an hour later. 'Call everyone,' I told her. 'The studio is open for business. Okay the old schedule with the church, and let's see if I still have enough students to fill the seats.'

I got Gaby up, dressed and fed, and delivered her to school. I was blessed that she was surrounded by loving friends, and at a progressive school that knew how to help her create a new definition of her life after Chris's death. Her teacher was love personified and gave my little girl a big hug. It was close to Halloween, and she was a true fairy princess. My fairy princess. Gaby smiled and said goodbye. Thank you, God, for making that easy.

I walked into the house and my assistant met me at the door. I stopped. Her energy was a bright light of excitement and joy. 'Everyone!' she said. 'Everyone but two people are back and starting next week.'

I remember thinking I should be emotionally overwhelmed, but I just kind of stood there, stunned. 'Everyone?' I asked. She responded by throwing her arms around me. We did a little hopping Irish jig in the entryway. 'You better get busy pulling scenes,' she commanded.

I did. Selecting the right material was the most important part of my job as a teacher. You could move people through their 'stuff' so much faster with material that pushed their buttons. It would usually take me hours to select just the right scenes for each person in my two classes. I went to the filing cabinet with its hundreds of stage and movie scenes, and stood there. I took a big breath to clear the panic attack. And I stood there a little longer. I had been gone for months. I didn't consciously know what was going on in their lives, didn't have the usual clues to guide me to scene choices. Again, from nowhere, that reminder wafted through me. 'Just Know.' So I opened the first drawer and, literally, it was almost as if the scene titles that I needed for each student were bigger, or illuminated, or – I can't really explain it. I just know they stood out from the rest. I was drawn to them. What had taken me hours before now was done in less than one.

I walked back to my office. 'You better get started, Dee. I have to take them to the copier tomorrow and ...'

'They're done,' I said in a daze.

'Huh?' was all she could muster.

'They're done.'

'How could they be done?' she demanded.

'I don't know how. I just knew what scenes to pick.'

It occurred to me that I was caught between the two worlds: one of not knowing and the other of knowing. But you can't know and not know at the same time. And I decided right there that I wanted to know. So I'd better choose that and stop thinking I didn't. So I did.

I wanted to Know. Everything. Even if I couldn't understand

it, or it was different from what I had believed, or I never knew it in the first place. If it was going to make my life process as easy as pulling these scenes, I was sold.

For the first time ever, I didn't feel so alone. I didn't handle loneliness very well. I equated it with being dead or with dying. I had often felt frightened and alone as a child, even though I had a mother and grandmother who cared deeply for me. Maybe we all feel alone. Ultimately. The human condition. But this 'knowing' felt like it had hooked me into a partnership with something greater. I liked it. I liked the connection.

The next week I walked into class and was met with lots of hugs and eager actors wanting to hear all the stories about shooting a film in a land far, far away with this great director and the star from *Back to the Future*. Hmm, back to the future. Now I know just how synchronistic that was.

So I told them about the wig, and showed them pictures from the set of me flying in the rig for the tunnel-of-light sequence. The stunt coordinator had even made a tiny one for Gaby so she could go up and 'fly like Peter Pan.' I told them how collaborative the crew was, and how they welcomed all my ideas. The most amazing story was going to the accounting office to settle up all my plane fares from flying back and forth to the States. 'It's Peter's gift to you, Dee. You don't owe us anything.' And how I had been filled with such love and appreciation for this loving bear of a man and a country that had supported me through one of my darkest times. In New Zealand I saw my first and only double rainbow. Yin/yang. Sweet/sour. Life.

During the opening hour's lesson, I proceeded to tell them about the voice in the night and the knowing. Something had shifted in me and this class was going to be different. I knew it. And I wanted them to go along for the ride, if they chose. I sensed that we would somehow move into an expanded vision of what an acting studio could offer. I didn't really know – and yet I knew. They could sense it and were ready. I was channeling as surely as

I did when acting, except I wasn't able to read my material even once. They acted their scenes, but I could now see more clearly where they were blocked and how to help move them through it. Our explorations moved very quickly from that point on. We had four auditors that first day back. Two of them joined the class. And that is how it usually went. For years, half the auditors would run for cover, and half would beg to join us. When the students were asked by the auditors to sum up the class, a favorite reply was, 'It's a great combination of God and fuck.' Or, we brought the spiritual into our everyday lives and made it work there. The process also revealed amazing insights about their psyches, too. Usually, they were astounded about the accuracy of these hidden gems. The auditors were sometimes dumbfounded by our approach.

Once, an auditor got up to do his scene – they had to partic-ipate – and a page into the scene I stopped him. 'What's your block about sex?' I asked. I could see his energy field pull back and he got a little defensive.

'Excuse me?' he said almost prudishly.

'Your sexual block. It's getting in the way here.' He looked bewildered. 'You know you have one, right?' When I got into this flow, or channeling, tact and gentility were dropped. There was a long silence. 'Okay,' I offered. 'There is a slight sexual joke in the third paragraph and you pulled away from your partner there.'

'I did not,' he argued. 'I didn't even move.'

'No, you didn't move physically. Energetically. Your energy pulled back from her into yourself.' His energy was so raw that we couldn't tell if he was going to attack me or crumble into tears. Fortunately, it was the latter. I gave him a moment to compose himself.

One of our macho guys jumped on stage, put his arms around him, and said, 'It's okay, buddy. It happens to all of us.' Then he added with a smile, 'She's a witch.' Laughter ensued. I asked if he would like to find out what was blocking him.

'Yeah,' he said. 'It's plagued every relationship I've ever had.' I instructed him not to say anything else. I didn't want any kind of suggestion to lead me astray. I had two of the students test with me. We always checked each other with muscle testing, or Kinesiology. Basically, we'd make a statement with a person's arm held out, and applied downward pressure; if it remained strong, it was positive or truthful. If his arm weakened, the statement was false. I usually used the same three students to test with, because I knew their 'arm strength' so well that the work went much faster.

When we began, I checked if I was going to an age. His arm remained strong. We narrowed it down to eight years old. Further testing confirmed that his father was the subconscious 'hook' into this issue.

He looked at me. 'Shit,' he said. 'That's when my dad left my mom.'

'Something sexual happened. Do you remember?' I asked.

'Sexual ...' he pondered. 'They were just screaming at each other. And then I saw his suitcase. He picked it up and left. I didn't see him again for a year.' We stopped. I saw a picture of his mother holding him. We balanced the energy around it with the statement, 'I am divine love.' I waited. After the energy is balanced, the information often comes flying out. It did. 'Oh my God. Oh my God!' he yelled. 'My mom grabbed me and said, "See, Jake! This is what sex gets you. Daddy has left us for some GIRL. Promise me you'll never do what Daddy did. Promise me you'll always be good to your wife."' He was sobbing at this point. A few students came to the stage for support. The final belief that Jake had put together that day at age eight was, 'When I really love a woman, I can't have sex.' This belief had already ended two engagements. I made him do the scene. He was brilliant. But I never saw him again.

You had to have guts to stay in class with this kind of probing.

And nothing was sacred. It wasn't for the shy, only for those who wanted to clear their emotional baggage and become better actors and people. One of my favorite longtime students lovingly recounted his first class: 'I had to dry hump my partner in a scene, get slapped by Dee, and renounce Jesus.' What he meant, in his own histrionic way, was that we ranged from spirituality and consciousness into exploring the human psyche as we delved into the raw emotional life of the material – wherever the chase would lead us. But in retrospect, it was the beginning of our quest as a group to close the gap between life and ourselves, and the One Energy: to create the knowingness that it is all one.

So it was by no coincidence that the Universe had delivered me to Spiritworks, whose motto emblazoned above the altar is: 'All Are One.' As the years passed, I was being drawn more and more into the energy of the church and the spiritual philosophy that it advocated. The Science of Mind belief that your thoughts create your life made sense to me. It had always seemed incongruent that we have no responsibility in what we have attracted into our lives, and that a Supreme Being out there was judging us and pulling the strings. That just didn't 'feel' right. Like an actor who knows a moment is false, that concept had never felt true with my own knowingness. What we were realizing in class was that false beliefs and perceptions poisoned our energy and led us to creating what we didn't want in our acting or in our lives.

I remember teaching a workshop in New York. One of the participants was a beautiful Midwest actress turned model. She had once been very successful, but recently had received more than one hundred callbacks for commercials and hadn't booked one of them.

'Not possible. There's a block,' I said. We began testing. We were led to *The 'I AM' Discourses*, a book we were often referred to by our Source. But no page number was cited. That told me that the basis of the block was a self-definition, such as 'I AM stupid,' or 'I AM not pretty enough.' We balanced whatever it was. By this time in our healing work, we knew to balance them *before* we tried to understand the block so as not to limit the energy we were balancing. In other words, we couldn't possibly know all beliefs, fears, and perceptions that made up the cobweb of blocks in our energy, so we balanced 'all,' and then got discernment around a big core issue. Next I was directed to the Life Subjects list, and specifically to 'Relationships.' (We had been channeling information about basic energy blocks that were inherent to everyone. Then we were given a list of genetic subjects, life subjects, and limiting core beliefs that we had compiled onto five different sheets.) 'There is a correlation between relationships and success,' I offered. 'Go back to when your dry spell started. What was going on personally?'

Again, and almost instantly, there was the gasping inhalation, a sudden realization, and then the tears came – the remembrance of truth. 'I met the guy I'm living with now. It was like love at first sight. We moved in together right away, and everything just kind of stopped career-wise.' We looked back further into her life. Every time she had a relationship, work stopped. She'd leave the relationship, and the work would start to flow again. It went back to her older sister. She had only heard the belief once, but it was from one of the Gods in her life and it stuck with her: 'I'm not going to work after the wedding. Working isn't healthy for a marriage. I have to focus on him.' And so was born the belief: I can't have a successful career and a good relationship at the same time. She was nine when that belief got rooted into her soul.

Three days later, I got a call from her. She had just booked a half-million dollar campaign for a beauty line.

Indeed, Spirit was guiding us to these insights. I was realizing more and more how accurate 'As you believe, it is delivered unto you' really was. The challenge was uncovering the core belief. So I began to listen to the Sunday lectures at Spiritworks and explore the lessons that were given. I brought some of these teachings into class, where I had bright students talk about the similarities to scientific principles, such as the spiritual belief of 'think only on these things' and the observer's principle in quantum physics: that a 'thing' only comes into existence when mind or consciousness focuses on it. I was also exploring different energy teachings and how they affected the flow of energy, like acupuncture, Reiki, Shamanism, and yoga breathing.

It occurs to me now that I had everything: a full acting studio, an acting career, a happy family life, time with my daughter, my health, and enough money to make life comfortable. During these unbelievable years, I taught four classes a week and did fifty acting projects. I even taught a film acting class at Gaby's fine arts high school. But, at the time, I couldn't see any of that as enough. My reality was still with the struggle and the 'making it.' Slowly, I was coming to the realization that this life process *was* the process: the tulips didn't get any more beautiful. You simply had to recognize and celebrate them. And that was the process we were discovering for ourselves: how to appreciate and celebrate and know that it's all in perfect harmony.

During these years, my focus gradually shifted more toward the healing work, and the patterns we were uncovering and clearing for the collective consciousness. As I had moved from primarily being an actor to a teacher, I was now defining myself more as a healer than a teacher. Little did I know I didn't have to separate them. They were all me. My one energy. And at some point, this shift scared me. Who was I, Deanna Bowers from Kansas, to think she could heal anyone? The answer: I was, simply, someone who asked the right questions. And I was receiving more information than I ever expected. Ask and you shall receive.

It was around this time that I was introduced to the pendulum, which is basically any object that dangles from a chain or string. You train your conscious mind to remove itself, so higher information can be discerned with this tool. The principle is the same as the divining rod that Native Americans use to find water underground. Just as an autonomic muscle response moves the rod downward, the pendulum can be tested for its 'yes' and 'no' movements – circular or back-and-forth, etc. – and used to respond to questions, much like muscle testing but solo.

I think if it had not been used by a doctor that I highly admired, using the pendulum would have been more of a stretch for me at that time. I mean, this was really woo-woo stuff for a Methodist girl from Kansas. But I could see the accurate results and the discernment she achieved with the pendulum. And I had asked for a way that people could heal themselves. So I gave up and expanded my horizons into accepting this tool. If it was going to help me with my Knowing, it was good to go. And it proved to be invaluable.

By this time we had been using muscle testing on a regular basis. The class had transformed itself into a healing venue as much as an acting one. And we were all aware that the acting or life journey and the spiritual journey were one and the same, and we were the only ones that kept separating them. After laboriously muscle testing for the highest limiting belief, we would 'clear' the energy: a process of tapping out negative beliefs and circling in positive ones, based on the Nambudripad system of releasing and curing allergies in the body. Basically, you placed both hands at certain points on your chest as you tapped yourself while saying the negative belief you wanted to release. Then you would circle your hands while stating the positive belief you wanted to replace it with. But it could take a half-hour with muscle testing to get through all the layers. And the pendulum was a tool that could be used individually. It made the work exponentially faster.

We began to see the patterns of limiting core beliefs that formed these blockages being altered as the energy was shifted. And we could absolutely witness the difference in people's lives physically and emotionally, and in their careers. People in class were going off medicines they had been on for years, leaving unhealthy relationships, booking jobs, or even leaving acting to become healers. Because they trusted me, and I trusted the voice, we were able to accept this work, and it was expanding our lives.

It could be a little harrowing, this mind expansion exploration. I would channel meditations and never know where they were going. One time a female student realized she had been molested by her father. Another got information around healing her cancer. One of my male students finally realized he was homosexual, and all his pain and sickness were really his own self-judgment. Somehow, as a family, we helped heal each other by being truthful with our own selves and each other. But we had to stay balanced for the truth to be heard.

That was the biggest breakthrough in the work: the day we realized we were not clearing and getting rid of anything – we were BALANCING energy. Scientifically, you can't get rid of energy; you can only change its form – for example, ice to water to steam. So we realized we couldn't 'clear' anything but, as nature does, we could choose to maintain the balance of energy which kept us out of reaction and into choice. When the energy was balanced, you could be in your knowing. If you were in reaction, you left creation and the ability to choose. We KNEW this in our acting – we had to start with a blank page of not knowing so that all knowing could come in. We knew that we had to let go of all the perceived blocks and choose to go anywhere the scene took us. We knew there could be no separation of self and character, and self and material; the character and the self were the same. But now we knew that all these concepts applied to life as well, and that we and God, humanity and God were the same. Acting, like life, was a spiritual process. And like nature, we must constantly rebalance ourselves, going from the torrential rains that wash away the old, to the droughts that dry us up, and back to the quintessential climate for our growth. And it is all a part of the One. That led us to one simple book that summed everything up for us: *The I Am Discourses.*

Basically, that book gives you permission and actually says that you MUST consciously direct the God energy for manifestation. You are God. All is the One Energy. If I hadn't walked through all the levels of this work before I read this book, I would have balked as surely as the new kid in class who doesn't want to do a sexual scene in front of everyone. It would have been too far out of my comfort zone. But this journey had been so clear, so precise, and so step-by-step that I could not deny the truth as written here: IT'S ALWAYS BEEN UP TO ME. I was given choice, and I'd better exercise that right. If I don't define the One Energy that I AM, who will? Unfortunately, the Collective Consciousness in its fear, judgment, and anger is usually the fallback answer. And so we began 'directing' our energy with the statement, 'I AM DIVINE LOVE.' No more tapping and circling. Just clear direction. And when we checked, the energy would be balanced.

This information was also changing my personal life dramatically. Gaby was now in her preteen years and challenging me almost beyond my 'limits.' Her hormones were ramping up, mine were slowing down, and it wasn't a pretty picture around the old homestead! I began using this conscious direction with our relationship and deciding what I wanted from it. And I taught it to her. Specifically, Gabrielle had been testing me by asserting her independence. She wasn't doing her homework on time, or to her ability. She was fooling around with boys she knew I wouldn't approve. She was defiant and argumentative with me. These are all typical displays of adolescent rebellion, but when they cropped up in my personal life, there was nothing 'typical' about them. It was causing me a lot of stress. Control has always been a big issue for me: if I didn't have control when I was young, my family fell apart. And so this was plugging me into childhood issues whose energy I needed to balance. This was actually an opportunity for both of us. I just couldn't get that perspective until I realized I was in reaction because of my own fears, so I was trying to micro-manage her to keep us safe.

I sat down with myself first and balanced my energy. Then I called my beautiful, defiant daughter to the room. 'What?' she demanded in a huff. I explained what I had learned about myself. Why I had been so controlling with her. I made it all about me. I told her that I loved her and knew she was smart and talented and would find her way. I was going to back off and allow her to make the mistakes that were hers to learn from. She looked at me for what seemed to be forever, and then threw her arms around me and started crying.

'But Mom,' she wailed, 'I need you to take care of me.' And in that moment it all became so clear: we had come together in this beautiful relationship to master our individual lessons of control and safety. I had to know that she created her own life. And she had to know it, too. After trying to control her and manipulate her into my idea of what a good little Valley Girl should be, I surrendered to the clear direction of 'I release you to your own DIVINE I AM self.' I posted it by my desk and on my mirror. It helped me stay in the KNOWING that she was creating herself perfectly. All the strife didn't end overnight, but we had an agreement to respect each other's life process. I allowed her to grow up, and in a way did that for myself. Gaby began to be more loving and responsible. It exponentially changed our lives in dramatic ways, not the least of which was her releasing the guilt for Chris's death and becoming her own creator. At the ripe age of fifteen, she was learning that she was the only one responsible for creating her life. Every choice was hers.

For years now, I had awakened on Monday mornings with excitement that I had another fabulous week of teaching ahead of me. But this new awareness made me realize my own responsibility to my acting career – or should I say the lack of one at this point. I had done a stage play and some fairly good guest-star TV roles, but I was dynamically aware now that I had not been consciously creating my career – except as a victim who thought she didn't have one. And I was going to change that now.

During one of my classes, we were having a lesson on self-creation and writing out what we wanted, etc. One of my students yelled out, 'Okay. So what do YOU want, Dee?' Since I had always wanted to do films, I think my spontaneous reply was interesting: 'I want a TV series with really good people, with great material, with decent hours so I can be with Gaby, and I don't want to have to audition for the network to get it.' I laughed and let it go.

Three months later I got a call to audition for a new pilot. 'It's comedy improv. Like *The Office*,' my manager said.

'But I don't do improv. And I'm known for drama.'

An enormous sigh of frustration wafted across the phone line. 'What would you tell your students to do?' she asked.

I paused. Damn. She got me there. 'I'd tell them to go play. All right. Send me the script for *Sons and Daughters*.'

She did. I went in to meet the producer/director who was a great guy. He explained everything about the set-up and the story; he wanted it real, for me to go into a range of emotions but to keep the comedy, etc. I did the audition. I felt really good about it. And I had a lot of fun doing it. As I was leaving, he said, 'By the way, you might not hear back from me right away. Because this is all improv, I have to edit the tapes and send them to the network. So you won't be getting a call to go in.'

I blinked – several times, I think. I recalled standing on the stage in my studio and claiming what I wanted that day. I'm sure I stammered. 'You mean … I don't have to go to the network.'

'Nope. It's kind of impossible with this kind of show.' At that moment I did the best improv of my life: I dropped to my knees and kissed his feet. When I was finished, I looked up at him with a huge grin.

'Well, I guess you're happy about that,' he replied.

I got the job. They even agreed to work around my schedule

with the acting studio. It was one of the greatest acting jobs I have ever had. Wonderful people, material, atmosphere. Improvisation is the acting equivalent of spiritually living in the moment: your moments affect the other actors and vice versa. You have to stay truthfully in your character as you create in each moment. Improv was always an emotional high for me, and I realized I had done it more often than I remembered. *Cujo*, in retrospect, had been filled with improv around the dog and the child. Moment to moment.

Sometimes it could get a little embarrassing. In *Sons and Daughters*, there was a scene where my daughter-in-law calls me a racist. 'I'm not a racist!' my passive-aggressive character answers belligerently. 'I dated a black man once.' Shocked, she inquires if I have ever told anyone. 'Of course not. I'm not stupid.' It was a hysterical moment. And then there was the scene where I have a heart attack at the end of a volatile argument with my son. I'd never had one or seen one. But I knew it. I just knew what to do. Channeling was awesome – in acting and in life. Again, I was in actors' heaven. And it was such a confirmation about healing work and consciously directing your energy with no expectations. Like a great scene, I had claimed the moment from the moment and then moved on to the next moment without expectation or force, and the Universe delivered me a perfect scene on the set and in life. As actors and people, we have to constantly balance our energy from fears and false beliefs so that we know and live our true selves, and when we do, the Universe responds.

The series only lasted a year. I guess I hadn't been clear about 'long-running' in my request. Before this healing work, I would have seen the glass as half-empty and gone into the 'Nothing ever lasts/All the good things go away/Why me?' scenario. Now I knew I just had to be more conscious to include that in my knowing. 'When life gives you lemons, make lemonade' is more than just a cute saying. Know. Turn your vibration into what you want with clear choice and direction. And call it all good.

The acting studio continued for another three years. One Monday morning I woke up and heard, 'Shit. I have to teach.' I stopped. I listened. I knew. This Camelot was done, and it was time to move on again. It was time to be Dee the actress, and to once again put my talents to the test. Four months later, with four full ongoing classes, I closed the Dee Wallace Stone Studio. I suppose I could have sold it. It was worth a lot at that point. But no one could do the healing work, and that had become as important a part of the studio as the acting. It was bittersweet. I loved each and every one of my students. After the last class, we partied till dawn in celebration of what we had shared and become together. But an entirely new chapter was about to be written in the big book of Deanna Bowers. And I was the writer now.

Chapter Twelve

I AM

Literally, I was the writer. I had been working on a book for years, correlating the channeled information about creating our own lives and 'what's it all about, Alfie?' It had gone through many rewrites as the information was constantly changing, and I simply didn't know if I was good enough to pull it all together. So I couldn't. Where was the 'me' that had already learned 'As you believe, it's delivered unto you'? Right. I knew it as an actress. I knew that when I auditioned in my power and with certainty, not only did I usually book the job, but I was peaceful when I left, knowing I had embodied the character. I believed in me to be the character, so I became the character, and the producers and directors responded. But this Knowing escaped me when I ventured into anything new. I kept looking outside of myself to see if I was okay.

I had put the book down in frustration and hadn't worked on it for months when I was invited to do a celebrity session with John Edward, the famous medium. I won't belabor the point about how this man is the real deal. I will simply say this: his people could have researched me for five years and never gotten the information that came through in that reading. Chris showed up and recounted stories that only we had shared, that not even our best friends knew. But the most important message was this: Get the book out. John kept saying, 'He's showing me writing. It's you writing. Are you writing something?'

I responded with a tentative 'Yes.'

'He's saying that you have to get this out. It's really urgent. You have to get this book out. His specific words are, "Even if you have to start all over, you have to get this out."' Chills ran up and down my spine, because when you hear the truth, you know it in your bones. I had to get past my smallness and fear and my not knowing, and use everything that I had learned and taught others to create this book for myself.

And so I did. Interspersed between acting gigs over the next year and a half, I worked with a very caring editor to help shape my first book, *Conscious Creation*. I was battered by so many fears and perceived limitations that at times I just wanted to give up. But that message from Chris helped keep me in my knowing, and the Universe had delivered this beautiful soul to help me finish it. How could I not follow through with it? Ultimately, I ended up self-publishing the book.

Several publishers were interested, but the feedback I kept getting was, 'I know this is the next big material, but my other editors "don't get it."' I heard those exact words from three different publishers. Trying to hold myself in balance, I asked for clarity around this feedback. Was there something within me that was blocking this moving forward? The answer was no. But I was directed to a particular paragraph in a book, and to a particular line, and that read: 'When you have information that is beyond what the collective can understand and is ready for, you will hear the words, "I don't get it."' I was stunned. I hadn't even read this reference book, so my subconscious couldn't have led me there.

'So what do I do, then?' I asked the voice, which I knew by now was I/my higher self/Universal Truth/God/my guides – well, The Everything. With its timeless humor, it responded with, 'Build it and it will come.' I laughed. I guess because I'm an actor it went to a film reference: *Field of Dreams*. Interestingly enough, Kevin Costner's character heard the voice, too! I chuckled. It's so easy to get it when you can laugh at yourself.

So with no steady job and no money coming in, I forked over a sizable amount of money to self-publish *Conscious Creation*. It was one of the most powerful affirmations I have ever made in my life, and I truly got to experience what real knowing was:

within me I knew the value and truthfulness of this book. No one had to publish it so I could know that. No one even had to read it for me to know it. What I knew was enough. And because I knew, I now receive emails daily about how this book has changed people's lives, so the knowing keeps rippling out and doing the very thing the book talks about: it raises the collective awareness.

It is interesting that after I made the decision to move ahead with the book, I was also moving ahead as an actor. I mean, I knew the meaning of 'As you do anything, you do everything,' but it was fascinating to see how it played out. Because I had decided to move ahead here, it shifted gears everywhere in my life. I was doing guest roles on some of the top television shows: *Saving Grace, Without a Trace,* and *Ghost Whisperer* to name a few. I was doing several independent films for which I would be paid a decent salary because I was a 'name' that helped get the project done. But I still tended to judge these indies as lower efforts, again seeing the glass half-empty and focusing on what was not happening instead of celebrating what was. Duh. I could write a book about consciously creating your life but I wasn't always living it. Why was I still refusing to take a drink when I had been led to the trough so clearly? Because life is simply a process of continual learning and expansion and choosing, and I just didn't get that; I was still judging the gifts and myself as not enough. I decided to change that. I chose to claim again all the points I had so clearly learned: stay out of judgment, keep my heart open, send out love, love myself, receive, trust, and know.

The Universe answered with an offer to do another horror film. And I didn't judge how it responded. I said yes. I said yes knowing that it was MY intention that this would be for my highest good in every way. And off I went to shoot Rob Zombie's *Halloween.* Rob was so real and warm and giving that you had no choice but to keep your heart open. I had a ball. I loved being on the set with my fellow actors. And it was never routine. I recall

doing a scene on the front stoop of the house. It was a complicated set-up with several 'extras,' children, and dogs. The entire
scene had to be carefully choreographed; it was in the wee hours
of the morning, freezing cold, and everyone had the creeping
crud. We rehearsed it over and over again, and I was getting
sicker and more frustrated as all the ghosts and goblins couldn't
remember where to go. I felt that old, familiar 'what-the-hell
sigh' welling up within me. Once it escaped, there was usually no
turning back. I excused myself to use the restroom, went to my
trailer, and looked at myself in the mirror.

'Okay. Are you going to replay this pattern?' I said. 'You
created this situation. You make the call. You want to lose it, or
have fun?' I stood there giving myself the good old Mexican
standoff. Then I smiled. For the first time on a set, I consciously
used my CHOICE to direct my energy the way I wanted it to
manifest, and not react from old addictive patterns.

When I got back to the set, I opened my heart, sat down, and
Scout Taylor-Compton and I started singing while we waited,
and having fun. We improvised fabulous moments, some of
which paid homage to the beautiful childhood of my own
daughter. 'Mommy, too tight,' a line from this scene that I had
suggested, was originally spoken by Gaby at age two and a half.
The next take went without a hitch. It was indeed a victory. I had
followed my creation technique and, like my acting one, I could
unconditionally rely on it to 'work.' I remembered how much joy
I had experienced in my earlier career and why I loved to act:
there was no bigger high than to experience a truthful emotional
expression. I had only been hired to do one day, and my agents
really weren't too enthusiastic. I had said yes anyway. One day
turned into three, and two weeks later I got a call. 'We need you
back on *Halloween*.'

'I already died,' I answered.

'I know,' the producer explained, 'but Rob wants to kill you
better.' I ended up making a sizable amount of money because I

said yes to a one-day shoot. You just have to trust the voice!

It was a violent and cruel death, and the first time you saw Dee Wallace, America's favorite mom, die on-screen. I didn't think much about that, until they had a screening for all of Hollywood's horror directors, and I got five calls directly after the screening. Basically, everyone had taken a rather large hit on E.T.'s mom being killed. But, as a healer, the irony didn't escape me. I had allowed my demons to be killed once and for all. I had brought my character's horror story to a close, as well as my own. It was fairly metaphorical, but I got it. It was done, and I could move on to other grander possibilities than the drama of torment. Wow. Thanks, Rob Zombie.

I had spoken to John Edward after the book was published, and he had encouraged me to begin doing workshops, no matter how many people came. The church had been very supportive in holding weekend seminars there. They had been growing in numbers, and the privates were also an extension of that energy. (Before I closed the studio, students had begun asking for private sessions to further explore what had come up in class. So, I began doing half-hour and hour healing sessions at my home.) I was now being invited on many talk shows, too, and was stunned at the hunger for and openness to the principles inherent in this work. People wanted to be healed, to be happier, more fulfilled, more successful, and healthier. It didn't hurt that I had a name and an instant built-in trust factor. And for the first time I didn't care if I used my status to help get this information out. I didn't have to separate the actress from the healer from the author from the mother from the lover, and I began to understand that when we do this, we are separating from or dividing up The One Energy: we are separating from ourselves. I could be it all. I wanted to be it all.

And one day I woke up and I KNEW I was the all. My all. And because I was MY all, I was THE All. I loved me. My heart was filled with my love for me. I acknowledged my celebration of me, and my knowingness that everything was good about me. My God. I was free. I felt like I could fly. I really liked this 'loving me' stuff, and it was different from narcissism. I wasn't looking into a mirror; I was looking into my soul. It felt empowering. This is what true power is, I thought: this expansion of love into the knowingness that you are safe and loved and honored – by you. And since you are God, by the big Kahuna him/herself. Wow. I was seeing the tulips, and they were awesome.

My passion from knowing this took over my life. I had to share it. I had to teach it. I longed to live there in every moment of my life. Every set I walked on became a joy, and every time I wrapped up a shoot someone would inevitably say something to the effect of 'Thank you for sharing your light.' Sometimes I would get a lesson I needed to move more into my knowing, and sometimes I would be there to give healing. That's how the Universe works: the perfect balance of giving and receiving. Or, as I like to call it, recigive. It's one thing. One complete circle: recigive.

For the first time I understood CONSCIOUSLY why life had been so good for Deanna Bowers from Kansas: she had trusted the Universe, expected good things, and believed in herself enough to trip off to New York and had fun going after her dream with passion and just said yes to what came along. I had done it all without KNOWING consciously, and yet knowing at some level all along. And now I could identify the process so I could always choose to create that in every moment and to guide others to get back to the true home in themselves. I was free. And it was awesome to fly.

Now, when something outside of me threatened to take away that freedom, I could rely on this process as I had with my beloved acting technique: I knew the way back. I knew it was ALL ABOUT ME. I could choose. I could know. I could direct. I could love myself. No one and no thing could take this away from me again. When the months came that the money was scarce and I had to dip into my retirement, I directed myself to choose: I know I am safe, taken care of, supported, and financially abundant. I was peaceful for the first time in my life around the fear of 'not having enough.' I was off that roller-coaster drama. I was free.

And so, as is sometimes the case when you decide to claim what you know, the Universe gives you opportunities to practice. It's the class called: Do you really know and are you sure in your knowing 101. People and situations show up to challenge us so we can choose, seek to rebalance, and further our knowing with these tests. It's the equivalent of stepping out whether you can see the net or not. You just have to know it's there.

Every once in a while a project would come along that would test everything I now knew, and would take me out of my Knowing – for a while. This one project comes to mind. It was three intense days with one other actor. Lots of emotion. Lots of energy. The director didn't know what he wanted, couldn't communicate his vision to us because he didn't have one, and we were floundering and frustrated because we couldn't give him what he didn't know. Much like the Universe feels about our confusion, I'm sure. Aargh! Between the exhaustion, the raw emotions, and the uncertainty, I lost it. Really lost it.

After two and a half hours of wrenching my guts out, he decided to play it 'less dramatically': 'We're going to do it all over again.'

I looked up at him, burst into tears, stomped my foot, and proclaimed, 'I won't do it!' and ran dramatically to my room. Gaby, in her most victorious of tantrums, couldn't have topped my performance. Eventually, we worked it out. But, whatever my justification, it wasn't how I wanted to treat anybody. And the biggest lesson I learned was to forgive myself for being human and love myself enough to just let it go. Most of the time, however, life was showing me that the very creation of me was being created differently. By me, of course. And life was manifesting in ever more joyous and miraculous ways.

I could see that I was seeing life, and therefore, creating life, differently. Because I was consciously choosing happiness and love, my life was reflecting that choice more and more. Two of my favorite stories relate this perfectly. For my birthday that year, two of my best friends took me to a spa where they had many healing classes designed to help you face your fears. I chose one called: The Equine Experience. I love horses. I am sure I was Annie Oakley in another life! To start, we were put through some interesting assignments that were eye openers, but my attention kept being drawn to a horse that the trainer seemed particularly worried about. When I inquired, he informed me that it was 'his baby,' and it had been severely sick with colic for days. I watched this big, burly cowboy hold back his tears. And there was the voice: 'Go work on the horse.' I mentally argued with myself that it wasn't my place, and that I had come here to learn.

'Go work on the horse,' it repeated. By this time I didn't argue with the voice. I followed guidance.

I walked over to the cowboy, explained that I did healing work, and that I thought maybe I could help the horse, and was that all right? He stared at me for what seemed an eternity. He was measuring my energy. 'Okay,' he said finally. 'Go for it.'

I approached the horse and gently said 'Hi,' and just stood there. 'Okay,' I said to the voice, 'what the hell am I doing?' I heard very clearly to put my hands on the horse. I balked. I had gotten this instruction twice before, but working with my hands was not really my expertise.

'So what's the problem? Afraid you DON'T KNOW?' The voice can be a pain in the ass sometimes. I put my hands on the horse, spoke gently to it, and closed my eyes. He didn't move. I just kept moving my hands where I was told, and feeling an immense love for this great animal. All of a sudden, I heard what sounded like a drain opening up. It was loud, and it freaked me out. Was I hurting him? I turned to the cowboy. 'Is that noise okay?' I asked.

'That's what we've wanted to hear for three days. It means his intestines are moving.'

'Keep working,' said the voice. I did. Then I instinctively asked the horse if he needed anything, and I was instructed to tell the cowboy to open his heart. Something had happened and he had closed his heart, and the horse had come forward to mirror this block with his own blockage to bring it to his attention. Swell, I thought, now I have to go say THAT? I did.

The cowboy looked at me, and tears welled up. 'Tell him "Thank you,"' he said. Wow – talk about hitting the easy button. I went back to the horse, delivered the message, and moved off to join my group.

They were in another corral, learning how to direct a horse purely by holding an intention and directing that energy from their solar plexus. At the end, we were to stand still and allow the horse to come to us. I must say that I was quite brilliant at directing and having the horse respond effortlessly. I ended and stopped, waiting for the horse to come over. He didn't move. I tried directing him silently with intention. The horse didn't move. I tried moving away to engage it. The same. Finally the female trainer suggested I go to the horse. 'No,' I protested. 'I want to know why he won't come to me. He came to everyone else!'

'Okay. Get down on one knee, take some deep breaths, and give up.' I did. The horse came over and nudged me. As soon as I surrendered, the outside energy could respond. I broke into tears. I needed this lesson again: 'Surrender, Dorothy.' After you direct, you surrender.

My second story changed my life because it was so apparent that my life had changed, and that I had changed. And I loved me for it. We were on our way to Christmas vacation with my family. You know by now, it is the most sacred time for me – being with all the people I love and cherish. The anticipation begins in October and snowballs into a frenzy of anticipation. So that is the energy we were holding when we arrived at the airport. My twenty-year-old daughter's boyfriend was going with us, and I was excited to show him the Bowers' Christmas Hullabaloo. He had never experienced a blowout like ours, where presents and food and drink and merriment run rampant. You never can see the base of the tree because the gifts reach out three feet.

We were standing on the curb, checking our bags, when I heard my daughter scream. I turned to see her boyfriend collapsing and going into a full seizure: eyes rolled back, his mouth starting to foam. She luckily caught him before he hit the ground. The first thing I remember doing was the work: 'I am divine love. I know. I know all is well here.' I knelt down and said to this almost unconscious boy, 'Integrate yourself; direct yourself to heal.' The people around me must have thought I was nuts. And then everything went into slow motion. People stopped. They put their coats over him. Someone called 911. The baggage handler collected our bags and put them aside. Someone picked up the tickets and driver's licenses that had scattered when I dropped them. An airline representative appeared. He informed me he would lock everything in his office, and handed me his card. 'Just let me know what you decide to do. I'll help in any way I can.' A friend had woken up from a sound sleep in Hawaii and called: 'You need something. What can I do?' He did a healing meditation. I called my healing partners: Do the work. The paramedics arrived in five minutes, loaded him inside, and off we went.

We arrived at one of the busiest hospitals in LA. The driver looked at me. 'You must have a guardian angel.' If he only knew. 'There are usually eight to ten ambulances lined up here.' We were the only one. They took him inside and started the tests immediately. I had called his father, who arrived and could furnish all the personal data I couldn't. I called the airline rep.

'We won't be flying today. I'll keep you posted.' I went over to console my daughter, who had been keeping her hysteria in check. This was her biggest nightmare: she had lost her dad, and the love of her life had been killed in an auto accident a year earlier. This was her first venture into trusting again. I looked at her, took her into my arms, and she crumbled. I reminded her to know. Know he was good, fine, and healthy. And know she didn't need to create being abandoned. Again.

Five hours later we left the hospital with permission for him to go on the trip as long as he took his medication and tests were done after vacation. I called American Airlines. The rep put us on a plane out the next morning, with instructions to call him upon arrival. We did. He had already checked our bags and changed our tickets to first class: 'My Christmas gift to you.' Someone came up to ask for my autograph. The rep looked at me. 'Are you someone famous?' I loved that he didn't know. He just did all this because … he did.

We arrived five hours later and had one of the best Christmases ever. And I told everyone about all the blessings and all the people who came forward to help and love us – like angels everyone was just there, even in their energy from far away. I was filled with awe, with love for the grace that was shown. I truly experienced as an adult what I had known unconditionally as a child: that I was taken care of. I knew what it felt like to be loved by the Universe, and I never, ever want to experience anything else.

Have I forgotten what I know since then? Yes. Have I been able to remember? Yes. Why? Because I choose the glory of that day over not remembering. I choose loving myself over judging myself. I choose knowing instead of confusion. And that is freedom. And that is the divine connection with The Energy that moves you into the experience that you are The Energy. We are all connected in this web of love and creation and oneness. And when we choose to surrender to that, there is nothing that can keep us from this truth: I Am Creation.

Appendix

1. Intention

Intention is a conscious focus of one's life energy. My overall Intention early in life to always be in 'my creative self' brought me everything that made me happy: singing, writing, dancing, acting, and teaching. As long as I chose the intention of joyful creation, everything seemed to be delivered to my doorstep. People showed up at the right time with needed information or to guide my career. Circumstances or synchronicities presented themselves to sweep me along into opportunities I couldn't even imagine.

This flow happened when I stayed in the moment and allowed the Universe to manifest according to its design, not mine, in its own time and in its own way, yet from my clear intention. And I was always grateful for the results. When I interrupted this flow with mental schemes, or tried to control or direct it, I sometimes got what my limited mind desired, but it was not what my greater spirit could conceive.

It might have appeared that my primary intention at any given moment was specific: I intend to dance, I intend to act, I intend to write, etc. But those secondary intentions really were all born from: 'I have to live from my creative center.' When our primary intent is to be in the moment and connected to the greater whole, the Creative Force, our secondary intent or desires are infused with extraordinary energy and lead to greater fulfillment.

When I held on to that intention, if one avenue wasn't the best choice, I would be guided effortlessly into another possibility that was more suitable and rewarding. I often wonder what my life would be like now if I had insisted on remaining a dancer even when it was obvious my creative life was in for a limited run. I certainly would never have had the opportunity to move millions of people in that little film called *E.T.*!

This spiritual or life lesson applies equally to the actor's craft or any creative endeavor. Doing an individual scene, or writing a chapter of a novel, or running a company, is simply a microcosm of the big picture: know what you want and let it unfold magically in its own more expanded way. If you break things down into too many specific ideas of *how* you think it should play out, the result becomes like most mental attempts in life: predictable, average, and unexciting.

The actor, writer, or corporate executive needs a clear intention, but the magic comes from living and being in the moment, unattached to expectations. Like life, each moment is new and you then have to deal with it truthfully and instinctively. We personally need a clear intention in life: to be love,   to be joy, to be fulfilled. But the magic of how that is delivered to us is released to the Universe for limitless expression of that intention.

When our intent or design is too specific, we risk losing our instinctual inspiration and often limit the multi-levels that creation might offer. When we get too specific about results, get into our heads and move out of our hearts, we often receive less of everything. When the actor, writer, or executive moves into total trust of his/her creative ability and its execution, he/she surpasses their own limitations.

When we, as people, move out of our fears into a total trust of the Universe, we are guided and led effortlessly into the magic of all possibilities. Some call it naiveté; others call it synchronicity. Nature doesn't think. It creates. The artless simplicity of life is living in the knowing, in beingness, and the trust of authentic truthfulness, a beautiful intention for a life production.

2. Beingness

Beingness is another word for the web of life or the world of nature from which we arise; it is our body's intelligence, the life force that drives us; it is our natural instinctive state of being. When we identify with our ego or mind, we cut ourselves off from its great power. Beingness is based in the moment; it is just what is, without design.

Fear is created from a focus on the past or on the future. It takes you out of the creative moment. In other words, when we are caught up in reaction to the past or projections of the future, we never create in the now. And the moment of 'now' is where all creation takes place. All acting or creative techniques urge you to 'be in the moment.' The few performers or creators that can achieve that surpass the material and become the material. So it is with life: when we can actually 'be' in each moment of our lives, beingness flows through us into the world and we become the creative material of life itself.

Its great edict is that we trust in our lives. Early in my career when I just trusted that the Universe would provide, all my needs were met: people showed up to help me; amazing opportunities appeared out of nowhere. The same applies to all the creative process. As creators, when we don't trust ourselves, we stand back and assess the material. We lose the connection and magic that 'being in the moment' creates, because the lack of trust invokes fear which forces us into control that blocks the flow. The false belief is: if we can control ourselves and thus control the outcome, we'll be safe.

But as in life, we never really have any control, and the fear that holds us in this false belief actually kills the moment of beingness where the magic of creation happens and things just materialize. With trust comes the knowing that 'it' will happen: money flows, loving relationships jell, our health improves.

When we let go of controlling the moment, we are in the beingness that creates it, and the past becomes irrelevant and the future nonexistent. This is when life becomes a constant surprise of unexpected creation.

When we invite our minds to be the conscious director of our clear intention and it chooses beingness over ego, mind serves its highest purpose. When we use our minds driven by fear as a safety net of control, it cuts us off from the beingness of the moment, and this limits creation's ability to provide us with all that we need or want. As an actor, when I surrendered to the uniqueness of the moment, the essence of the scene was discovered and I channeled its highest creative expression. When we surrender to the uniqueness of our own beingness, we are guided effortlessly on our magical journey through life.

Our emotional wounds are our stories, our baggage that keeps us tied to our mental safety nets of control and fear. When we can live in the creative, joyful light that is our authentic self, we cast those nets aside for the wings of flight into all possibilities.

3. High Energy

Everything is energy, and the universe is one continuous energetic whole. However, our perception of reality breaks this whole down into compartments that separate things, and creates divisions in ourselves. We become identified with lower and higher, inside and outside, with different levels of our being like the emotional and mental self, and we become separate from the unity of ourselves and the web of life around us.

The essence of Charles Conrad's acting technique, which can be applied to all creative endeavors, was to have us 'raise' our energy from the mental plane to our spirit essence, but was in fact a method for us to identify with this whole and allow it to interpret the material from a broader unified perspective. From here we had access to information not readily gleaned by our senses. Many of his students came to realize that this approach applied to our understanding of life as well as acting.

You would read a scene to understand the map, to scope it out, as it were. Then you'd fold up the map and step into the moment where the mind stops and you identify with the whole and move with its flow of energy. Let's say you're driving from California to New York; it's good to know the best route to take. But within that framework, you also want to enjoy the scenery, experience the various encounters along the way, and be prepared for any unexpected change of plans. If a relative calls along the way and you want to see them, you adjust your plans and take a side trip, which may lead to another adjustment. In other words, the best scenario is to have a plan and then dance with the unexpected in the moment. You have to allow the trip to take on a life of its own. And if you have to be in New York at a specific time, or need to arrive at a mark on the stage or set on a particular cue, your internal travel guide compensates and gets you there on time or at the exact moment your partner arrives.

Nature is not a machine or even a giant computer, but is more like an organic being whose parts blend together instinctively. A tree has the intent to grow in such a way as to gather as much direct sunlight as it can, but doesn't think about how to position its branches; it just senses the light and moves toward it. When we allow ourselves to create an intention but be energetically moved by instinct, trusting in our knowingness, our songs of life are unique to us and in tune with everything around us. We are, literally, drawn to the light.

We become high energy, as opposed to how we act or live when we are driven by mental concepts of how to realize an intention, which are usually based on perceptions from the past or projections about the future. Pure energy just vibrates differently than manipulated energy. Pure energy, like nature, is truth in being. It directs the journey and the creation, and we step aside to be in the experience. It is life connecting with life by bypassing the mental realm.

In any expanded creation, as in living, the mind can actually – must actually – choose to relinquish its plan of action. It serves the One Energy by creating the map of freedom and then stepping aside to allow the unexpected, the field of all possibilities, to come into play. This frees us from predictable results into all possible outcomes.

4. Judgment

Judgment is the mind's chief tool to create separation between the living moment and us. As we've seen, being in the moment and out of the ego and mind is how we connect to the greater part of ourselves and to all of creation: us as limitless creators of endless possibilities. Judgment is how the socializing forces of family, school, and religion can rob us of that spark, which is our innate connection to God.

While growing up, we all hear judgments about 'other' people, races, or religions, and how special we are and how wrong they are. Even worse, we hear what's wrong with us: we're too pretty or too plain, too quiet or too loud, too smart or too average. And as I learned after my dance recital, we are judged if we celebrate our uniqueness, our special quality. Our spark of the divine.

For some, this creates a permanent breach with their greater whole or self, as they go through life locked in their minds and critical of themselves and everyone around them. Judgment is the refuge of those whose heart centers have been wounded and closed down. It becomes a defense for our own self-worth.

Whenever we move into judgment, of ourselves or of others, we automatically separate our energy from the One Energy that creates and organizes everything, from flowers blossoming on cue to the dance of star clusters. We eke out a mental existence, big or small in relative terms, but never acquire the treasures of mind, spirit, talents, and abundant prosperity that await those who ask and expect to receive.

If I had judged myself as unworthy, I would have never been able to ask for my trailer on the set of the movie *10*. Those fears of 'not being good enough' were yet to be reactivated, and so I joyously could come forward and claim what I wanted. I could show my religious film to ten agents because I didn't judge them as too insensitive to see my talent through any medium. My naiveté, or childlike openness, was keeping me in life's flow, expecting that the Universe would take care of me. And it did.

When we live our lives from a place of damage control – 'What if?/Maybe I shouldn't/What do I know?' and (my mother's favorite) 'What will others think?' – we are choosing the perspective that life is dangerous and we have to manipulate it. That is a negative intention (making sure I don't get hurt), which takes us out of our oneness with all energy and throws us out of balance. We move into reaction instead of creation, focused on what we DON'T want, instead of asking for what we do want.

'To thine own self be true' and 'As you believe, it is delivered unto you' are the two components that encourage us to stay in non-judgment through any test: what your heart tells you is your truth, and however you believe you will create. When we apply both of those precepts to any situation, it removes the fear that pushes us into judgment. We make a clear choice to believe the highest and best choice from love, and move confidently into creating the lives we want and allowing others to do the same.

The secret is to say YES to life. Without fear that demands judgment, we say 'Yes!' To a life of love, joy, and unlimited creation.

5. Instinct

Emotion is driven by mental concepts; instinct is a still, small voice of individual guidance that often is accompanied by a small shift in energy. In everyday life a hunch or intuition about people and situations is usually an instinctive response, which bypasses the mind's reliance on past history or future plans, to respond in the moment. And since it's more primal, it is connected to the web of life and is broader in scope than mere analysis.

Children naturally respond instinctively and it's from that place that their celebrated 'knowingness' comes from. But, as we grow older, our egos are shaped from societal influences; concepts of right and wrong and the fears they generate replace our instinctive sense of things. We become mental beings whose futures are dictated by our histories to create socially acceptable futures. And we are taught to tame natural instincts to that end.

This was clearly demonstrated to us in Charles' acting exercises where we were all given the same scene and asked to prepare it over the course of the week. Everyone had basically taken the identical approach – the good but safe mental rendition of the material.

The following week we were all given another scene in class, told to read it with our partner, and then put it down. They were all original, based on an actor's instinctual response from their unique knowingness. Instinct allowed us to create from our blank page; the mind gave us computer readouts of collective averages. Instinct keeps you in the moment of now, and of all possibilities.

Instinctual knowing has a broader perspective and tells us when a situation or opportunity fits into a more comprehensive scheme of things. This was evident when I decided after doing the movie *10* to do a favor for a director, an instinctive response that brought a heart result: meeting my future husband Christopher Stone. Or, when I followed my guidance about doing the horror film *The Howling*, which forced me to start facing my fears, and it opened up a genre that would feed my career for decades.

Instinctive reaction is allowing you to take action when you hear your voice of higher knowing. When I've trusted that voice, despite my own fears or any outside influence, it has invariably proven to be an accurate guidance system leading me to innovative and creative explorations that broaden my life's scope. Inherent in the risk of instinctual trusting is that it always creates the ultimate safety.

6. Heart

Feelings come from our heart center, while emotions are usually generated by a mental concept. And it's one way we process what is happening, not only within us but also in the outside world. You hear yourself saying, 'I've got a feeling about that,' or have a healer ask you 'What is the feeling tone?' of a particular experience or memory. It's the heart's brain feeling its way to an understanding of a situation, and usually with much finer discrimination than the mind can ever attain.

When our feelings 'get hurt' and we negatively react to something in our lives, instead of 'feeling our way to an understanding,' we often close down our heart center to protect ourselves, and automatically shift into a mental assessment mode. We falsely believe that we are safe from harm, because we are now in a separate mind space where we can be completely 'objective.' Or, where we manipulate everything to fit some preconceived idea of how it should be.

But, by shutting down our hearts and withdrawing our web of feelings, we sever our connection to deeper parts of ourselves and those parts of others. Like the connection between parent and child, it's how we get nourished by the exchange of energy through love and acknowledgment. So, when we close down our hearts, we cannot give love or receive it; we cannot acknowledge others or have them acknowledge us. The exchange of energy shuts down.

When I got caught up in the negotiations with Universal Studios over *E.T.*, it triggered an emotional reaction, the ego mind claiming its territory and protecting its interests. I was willing to walk away from a great script and a great part in a movie I instinctively knew would affect the lives of millions, all because I wasn't being paid enough. I saw it only in terms of acknowledgment, and what that meant for my self-worth. But acknowledgment must come from within us before it can truly be received outside the self.

A self-assured happy woman, secure in her own self-worth, might have handled these issues differently. Instead I reacted from fear, from a lack of self-love, which only created more fear and cut my connection to myself and the greater whole or the Universe. This is not to excuse the behavior of others, only to acknowledge my part in the ensuing drama, and to understand that the heart is sufficient unto itself, and living from that center is its own reward.

For the actor, when you pull your energy back into yourself 'to be safe,' you disconnect from your partner, from the material itself or the greater whole and begin to manipulate yourself and others, and the result is a secure but surface acting experience. You've left your blank page, lost your spontaneity and ability to create from a deeper part of yourself. You've lost your heart energy and its ability to connect and create truthfully. You stop feeling.

This also applies to our daily lives when we don't connect to others from a heart space, whether it is the waitress at the coffee shop or our child's soccer coach. Choosing to be in your heart space, and out of reaction, shifts others into that same space and creates harmony. You create a bridge to another person because the heart doesn't recognize separation; it is one, and you become one under its guidance.

7. Sending Out

Giving is receiving is an ancient concept and part of many religious traditions, including that of tithing. Whatever you give – usually money in some charitable context – is returned unto you tenfold. But, while many of us give at work or at church or synagogue, our hearts are closed to most but our immediate circle of family and friends. We don't connect or send that heart energy out to the world, or become intimate with strangers or those foreign to us, and thus become isolated from the greater whole of humanity.

For creative people, writers and actors and others, this also applies to the business end of their professions, or the business people, I should say. They often operate from a different set of principles and priorities than the artist, and because of that they often don't feel 'received' by their counterparts. Everybody closes down their hearts, hides behind mental protections, and becomes reactive instead of giving.

This is what happened on *E.T.* Both sides in the monetary and billing disputes were not open to the other's position or sending them any heart energy, and so each became reactive. We took ego positions, claimed our turf, and when forced to accept terms, retaliated. Ironically the film itself became a great artistic and monetary success; the audience received the heart energy the artists sent out, and gave back tenfold.

We all know when our hearts are open and we're sending out love. We feel good; we expand. The key is that this is always our choice. But all too often, we allow outside circumstances to dictate our heart response. We wait for the money to show up before we send out the love that creates the money. We wait for our beloved to unconditionally love us so we are safe to commit our hearts. We shut our heart light off to protect ourselves from hurt or abuse.

When I opened my heart and could again connect during the filming of *Cujo*, it was because the outside circumstances encouraged its expression. It wasn't me getting back to me, regardless of what I was receiving, but me being able to rekindle my light because I was being taken care of again. I still had to learn the choice was mine. When we move into consciously creating 'us' regardless of what 'they' do, we move out of reaction and into creation. We choose to live with an open heart in balance and choice.

8. Reception

To receive what the bountiful Universe is sending us, we must be open and clear: allowing the energy to come to us without emotional prejudice or mental judgment. It is accepting whatever is delivered unto us without conditions. In this way we become part of the flow back and forth with All That Is; the circuit is open; we give and receive, and our true needs are fulfilled.

When an actor receives the impulse energy sent by their partner, it affects them and changes them in that moment. They have the choice of responding from their heart or feelings and making this a truthful exchange – making it 'real', as Charles would say. Or, they can think first, categorize it according to past experience, and then react to that idea and break the circuit of exchange with their partner. It then becomes a 'me' moment, not an 'us' moment.

In life, we need to experience our heart response of positive self-creation first, and then consciously choose to direct its manifestation. That is how the Universe, as our partner, will respond in the creation of our lives. Its guiding principle is the energy of directed love or connectivity. So the technique is turned back on us. We don't react; we create from choice. We choose the direction, get a response, and consciously choose another. In this way our giving is receiving, and our receiving is giving, creating an unbroken circuit with the Universe.

When I constantly moved into reaction around the challenging situations that my beliefs were creating in my life, I was operating from my emotional center, creating a me/them scenario that placed the blame on other people or outside circumstances. I refused to see my own responsibility in their creation, and from there I couldn't make choices that would shift me and, ultimately, shift my life out of negativity.

This continued despite my attracting situations that so clearly pointed out this dynamic. For instance, I was in reaction over the fallout from *E.T.*, about a self-aware alien whose heart light was always on, and so I get *Critters* for my next film, alien fuzz balls wanting to eat me alive. If that wasn't enough, the transformation – interior and exterior – from *Together We Stand* to *Nothing Is Easy* should have been painfully obvious to anybody with a modicum of self-awareness.

I stopped receiving from the Universe, shut my heart down, and closed myself off from the energy of creation. Operating from the heart, out of mental reaction, guides us to our individual truths. Then we must choose to objectively see our part in the creation of our lives and to take responsibility for it. When I stopped reacting and opened my heart, life shifted for me and ultimately the pattern was revealed: wherever I went, there I was. It was about me all along. I had to choose.

9. Zero Point

The Zero Point is the place of nothingness from which all possibilities can be created: the blank page that Charles always talked about in class. It is without the baggage of past history, present manipulation, or future expectation – the zero charge of the infinite now. It is the intersection of beingness with our clear intent from which we can give form to an original personal expression in this moment in time that will never come again.

In acting, when we have the courage not to plan every moment for safety's sake, we open ourselves to the collective experience and knowledge of all peoples of all times, a greater pool of information than our limited minds could ever access without this channel. We saw this countless times in class, where a student who didn't know the character was crippled became crippled, who had never studied a dialect spoke it perfectly.

We actually experience the moments as they happen, so the exchange on-screen is real and raw and exciting. We've all experienced this reaction with a sudden surprise, or seen ourselves act more quickly than imaginable in an emergency. Some say that it's an instinctive response, or that we give ourselves permission to be excused from socially accepted behavior in the moment. I think that this zero point not only summons infinite possibilities, but all of our many selves.

When I gave up and surrendered to my fertility zero point, I finally got pregnant. This opened my heart and not only led to the creation of a baby but also a deep personal and professional acceptance after years of trying to create present success from past failure. That allowed me to let go of all my old definitions of myself, life, and others; these definitions were not allowing me to move onto the blank page where nothing had been written and everything was possible. We cannot create by recreating.

When we keep defining ourselves by past disappointments,

we perpetuate those very limitations in the present and into the future. Events happen to show what we need to heal, but many of us choose to keep our 'story' alive as a banner to our victimhood. We need to heal and forgive the old wounds and release these definitions, and embrace our unlimited potential. It is in being born anew each day that ultimate creation of our lives happens, from the zero point to the infinite in every moment.

10. Surrender

Surrender is the highest choice we can make: it is the choice to give up our will or control of things, and to allow the influx from the greater whole or the Universe to come in, and for us to create anew from what is given. If we don't surrender, whatever the circumstances, we divide the One Life Force into two separate energies warring within us and against each other, and we create a 'house divided against itself.'

As actors, if we fight the material, our partner, the director, or the studio, we break the flow of the One Energy into opposites that cannot create one whole. We argue for separation and limitation and we get both, in the present and the future, as entrenched beliefs that keep recreating the same results. When I kept fighting the business people, I kept driving the business away from me. I wasn't embracing the whole energy needed to forge the career I wanted.

As I surrendered and allowed the Universe to gift me with teaching, where the circuit of energy between my student and me was an unbroken whole, I could be led along my road of personal healing back to the home or the soul that I Am. I could stop fighting myself and others, open my heart, move back into trust, and allow the flow of energy to move again into my acting career. The unbroken whole in whatever form is a metaphor for the mind of God.

When we begin with the pure knowing of a still mind and heart, and then surrender to its highest manifestation, the results are far more creative, innovative, and expansive than when we allow our fears to dominate our creative efforts. We are then safe enough to begin creation from the nothingness of the blank page, instead of recreating past efforts. At death there is always new birth, and vice versa. The One Energy is forever expanding.

11. Knowing

Knowing is our natural state of grace that is beyond trust, hope, and belief. It is the acknowledgment of our connection to All That Is, or God, and as a result everything is in perfect harmony. We are the One Energy. To Know is to Be and to be at peace with all manifestation. Love for self – and ultimately others, as aspects of the One – is true Knowing.

As an actor, I must know the material and character as an extension of my own being, not out there but within myself. As such, I know beyond a doubt that I can do a certain part because I become it. That Knowing is so complete that it balances any fears I may have and carries me into total commitment to the material. When I Know it, everybody knows it, from the casting director to the eventual audience.

When we truly Know that *we* are 'the material' of our lives, our commitment becomes so complete that our fears are consumed by our love of the creation that we are. We know it has always been us, and we are secure in directing our manifestation and accepting responsibility for all that we create. We see the beauty in the lows and the highs and know that they are good.

Our Knowing helps us forge ahead without fear, and that enables us to create our dreams and accept what manifests as its perfect expression. When I created a strong intention, it would often manifest as something different from what I expected but appropriate for all involved. The state of knowing was matched with clear direction, and created the highest outcome.

When the stakes are high enough – a child in danger, for instance – it is easy to move into the state of unconditional Knowing: you have to save the child. Our quest is to choose to Know without cause or proof triggered by anything outside of us. When we come from Knowing, we send that Knowing out to the Universe; it responds to us and we are free.

12. I AM

Knowing that You Are Creation, the I AM, eliminates fear because it eliminates the illusion of separation. The All knows no limitation. Knowing you are the I AM, or Universal Energy, allows you to create through partnership, instead of reacting from a victim's mentality. You are no longer at the 'whim' of the world. You move into the empowering energy of taking responsibility for the direction of your energy and its surrender, and therefore your life.

When I do a part as an actress, I learn my lines, then I surrender to that inner actor within me who moves in rhythm with the totality of all that is happening in the scene. My trust of creation allows all the elements to dance in harmony together. The moment fear enters into this process – fear of not being good enough, of not meeting others' expectations – it becomes about control, instead of trust and knowing. Creation becomes less joyful and limited.

The Universe works the same way. When we Know unconditionally that we are the Creative Force, we can then trust the harmony and unlimited opportunity afforded our creation. We are in the flow of all that is. When we own that all other energy is also the Creative Force, we move into allowing everyone to create and define all energy through the choice of their own individual expression. There is no separation; there are simply different choices. And it is all Creation.

The challenge is continually to choose to Know that I Am, and as creation – the source of all that is – how can we not receive what we need? When we ARE the I Am, there is nothing to fear because we know we create everything. We realize we are the ever-expanding creative energy of the One. And we are free and totally taken care of.

Bibliography

Hawkins, David R. *Power Vs. Force.* Sedona, AZ: Veritas Publishing, 1995.

Lincoln, Michael J. *Messages from the Body.* Cool, CA: Talking Hearts, 2006.

McTaggart, Lynne. *The Field.* Boston, MA: Element Books, 2003.

Ramtha. *Ramtha: The White Book.* Yelm, WA: JZK Inc., 1999.

Saint Germain. *The 'I AM' Discourses.* Schaumburg, IL: Saint Germain Press, 1987.

Talbot, Michael. *The Holographic Universe.* New York, NY: Harper Perennial, 1992.

Walsch, Neale Donald. *Conversations with God: Book One.* Charlottesville, VA: Hampton Roads Publishing, 1995.

Dee Wallace has worked as an actress in film, television and the stage for over thirty years and with some of Hollywood's biggest names, including Steven Spielberg, Peter Jackson, Wes Craven, Joe Dante, and Blake Edwards.

Her 135 feature film credits include such classics as *The Hills Have Eyes, The Howling, Cujo, 10, The Frighteners,* Rob Zombie's *Halloween* and most notably her starring role in one of America's most celebrated films, *E.T. The Extra-Terrestrial.* Dee has starred in four television series and had had numerous guest star appearances on such recent hit shows as *Grey's Anatomy, Cold Case, Without a Trace, Ghost Whisperer, My Name is Earl,* and *Saving Grace.*

As an author, Ms. Wallace has written two other books devoted to the art of self-healing: *Conscious Creation* and *The Big E.* She has been featured on various show formats with Byron Katie, Gary Zukav, Neale Donald Walsh, and Michael Beckwith. Her call-in radio shows air worldwide. She conducts monthly workshops to introduce people to the healing techniques outlined in her books, and facilitates numerous private healing sessions at her office and by phone. Her website: www.officialdeewallace.com. *Image Productions, 818-876-0386.*

John Nelson is the author of *Starborn, Transformations, Matrix of the Gods,* and *The Magic Mirror,* the 2008 COVR winner for the best New Age book of the year. He is the former editorial director of Bear & Company and Inner Oceans Publishing. In this capacity he has acquired and/or edited such titles as *Maya Cosmogenesis 2012, Expanded Medicine Cards,* Jean Houston's *Mystical Dogs,* and Barbara Marciniak's *Family of Light* and *The Path of Empowerment.* Mr. Nelson is the owner of Bookworks Ltd. and has recently edited such titles as *The Sacred Promise* by Gary Schwartz, *The White House Doctor* by Connie Mariano, *The 12-Step Buddhist,* and *God is Not Dead* by Amit Goswami. His website: www.johnnelsonbookworks.com.

BOOKS

O is a symbol of the world, of oneness and unity. In different cultures it also means the "eye," symbolizing knowledge and insight. We aim to publish books that are accessible, constructive and that challenge accepted opinion, both that of academia and the "moral majority."

Our books are available in all good English language bookstores worldwide. If you don't see the book on the shelves ask the bookstore to order it for you, quoting the ISBN number and title. Alternatively you can order online (all major online retail sites carry our titles) or contact the distributor in the relevant country, listed on the copyright page.

See our website **www.o-books.net** for a full list of over 500 titles, growing by 100 a year.

And tune in to myspiritradio.com for our book review radio show, hosted by June-Elleni Laine, where you can listen to the authors discussing their books.

MySpiritRadio

DEE WALLACE is a must EXPERIENCE. She is a spiritual archaeologist that helps you dig at core issues. Whether it is live, print—as in her compelling spiritual memoir Bright Light*—or via the web, her healing words and energy will help you to excavate core truths to live a more balanced life. Many teach . . . but only a few can help others to transcend.*
John Edward, host of CROSSING OVER and co-founder of INFINITEQUEST.com

When you know Who You Are, you understand that all energy is from the creative force, that there is no separation, only choices to be made. Dee Wallace is an inspiring actress and teacher who has learned how to apply this empowering energy to her art, and has written this extraordinary book for those who wish to learn from her wisdom and apply it to their lives.
Neale Donald Walsch, author of *Conversations with God*

Dee Wallace is the real deal; irreverent, focused, and profound; she will shift you in the blink of an eye. This amazing book reflects that bight light, illustrated through the words and the wisdom contained here. It will guide you to shine brighter than you ever thought possible. Read this today if you are ready to fundamentally shift into balance and joy.
Jennifer McLean, Author *The Big Book of YOU, Healer & Host of Healing with The Masters*

Dee Wallace puts a mirror to her heart as she shares her deeply profound insights into acting, life and spirituality. Bright Light *is a remarkable portrait of love and awakening, with valuable lessons for every reader.*
Geoffrey Hoppe, international author and spiritual lecturer

In this glorious book, Dee Wallace inspires us to show up in our lives as our authentic selves. Dee teaches through sharing her own story of how she succeeds by being herself at all times, and she displays for us the courage it takes to live authentically no matter the cost. Bright Light is delightful read that feels as though she is speaking directly to our hearts and our lives.

Sheila and Marcus Gillette, authors of *The Soul Truth: A Guide to Inner Peace, The teaching of THEO*

Everyone is born in the Light and Light takes the form of unique gifts. Few are the Souls who use their gifts to let their Light shine. Dee Wallace—through her extraordinary journey as an actress, movie and television star—has used every experience in the creative process to deepen her awareness of LIFE. This empowering book speaks of the journey and points the way . . . a must read for all creative Souls.

Harry Morgan Moses, D.D.